A Monk in the Bee Hive

A Short Discourse on Bees, Monks and Sacred Geometry

by

Skye ann louise Taylor

A MONK IN THE BEE HIVE:
A SHORT DISCOURSE ON BEES, MONKS AND SACRED GEOMETRY
by SKYE ANN LOUISE TAYLOR

LOGOSOPHIA

Copyright © 2020 by Skye ann louise Taylor

Logosophia, LLC

Logosophia, LLC
90 Oteen Church Road
Asheville, NC 28805
www.logosophiabooks.com
logosophiabooks@gmail.com

Library of Congress-in-Publication Data

Taylor, Skye ann louise
A monk in the bee hive: a short discourse on bees, monks and sacred geometry

ISBN 978-0-9815757-7-3

Distributed by Small Press Distribution
Non-Fiction
1. Spirituality   2. Apiculture   3. Ecology

Book design by Susan L. Yost
Cover art by Sage Kovacs

This book is dedicated to all
who cultivate kindness

and to Chief Seattle whose words
have inspired many of my own.

ACKNOWLEDGEMENTS

It took six years to write this short book and many people supported me along the way. Living as a monk outside the container of a monastery is a challenge in our very busy, productive and driven society. The simple life is so often mistaken for laziness yet is it far from that. It is a rigorous and solitary life that yet depends upon others, as all people and things depend upon each other. Even a solitary life is not an independent one.

First and foremost in this regard I must thank my benefactor Nancy Weber for her constant support, both financial and in trust of my work.

TSL of Hudson, NY offered me the first opportunity to present Temple Hive at their lovely cultural center, and I thank Linda and Claudia for that.

Claudia and Carolyn Eden both read the book as it came into being, while Jonas and Sarah, ever supportive, became as family to me. Gunther Hauk mentored the hive design and encouraged me to write.

My high school teacher Miss Spencer first woke me up at my desk in the back corner of class, interweaving history, music and literature, breathing life into learning. My college teacher Roger Freeman taught me to solve problems by making them 3D, not merely spun thought forms.

I would be remiss if I did not acknowledge the inspiration and information gleaned from many authors over the years of preparing this book. They include Fritjof Capra: *The Tao of Physics*; Lyall Watson: *Rhythms of Vision*; Arthur Koestler: The *Roots of Coincidence*; Immanuel Velikovski: *Worlds in Collision*; Jerry Mander: I*n the Absence of the Sacred*; Rudolph Steiner: *Bees*; Jurgen Tautz: *The Buzz about Bees*; Rowan Jacobsen: *Fruitless Fall*; and Rose-Lynn Fisher's beautiful photography in *Bee*. There are many others of course and I wish no slight by not remembering them all! Thank you all for following your hearts.

Finally I wish to thank my publishers, Krys and Steve of Logosophia. They have offered a number of books that meld the sacred with our natural world and I recommend you seek them out. I feel this work has fallen into the right hands, including yours I trust.

May the blessings of the natural wonders of this world fill your life.

Table of Contents

PREFACE

Profound meditation—Zen, Tibetan, healing, or otherwise—has not rendered Skye ann louise Taylor into a garden-statue Buddha, beatific but inert. Rather it has made her fearless in her priorities, uncompromising in her compassion and an astute observer. With affection and her lyrical, humorous descriptions, she introduces us to the beehive and its citizens: Her Majesty the Queen, worker girls, and the lumbering drones. Skye's understanding—gathered through seasons of care taking and tender, silent attention—is offered to us in a few short chapters, fascinating yet poignant in the face of our reckless disruptions of bees' well-being.

Skye explores the integration of sacred geometry, the natural environment within the beehive and our own internal landscapes. Her knowledge of natural patterns, gathered through years of study, became brilliantly relevant in observing the behavior and needs of bees. Her meditation, honed through years of Zazen discipline, allowed activities of bees to arise undisturbed. In stillness, her perception clarified itself into insights, wonderfully expressed in her writing, which make it possible for us to journey with her into the realm of bees.

Skye is a tough-love mother who wants us to see and appreciate, and to reconsider our conduct in terms of bees, the environment, and our own inner awareness. It is not difficult to envision the moments when she describes her fury (and heartbreak) after carelessness causes carnage in the hive, but the integrity of her compassion embraces harmer and harmed alike. *A Monk in the Bee Hive* is a revelation of natural cooperation and its corresponding outflow of benefit, not just as honey, propolis, and pollination, but as a guide to how we might find new accord in a degenerating world.

Chagdud Khadro
Khadro Ling, Tres Coroas, Brazil

AUTHOR'S NOTE

Staying for a few months in Rishikesh in 1977, I lived in a round hut in a compound called 'Swiss Cottage', a little out of town and close to the river. Here the Holy River Ganga gushes out of the foothills into the great plain of India and the job of the village is to protect her. A few miles up-river another branch joins in the frothing turbulence and where their waters meet a small monastery sits, caring for this particular place, this particular confluence of rivers. The teachings offered here are woven into a curriculum that includes astronomy, mathematics, music, meditation, gardening, medicine, astrology and design. Though invited in, I did not accept the offer to stay for seven years. I did not think I had the time. I was 26 years old. Instead I went to America and got caught up in many ways, gradually learning a little of all these subjects over the next forty years. If I had accepted, I would have understood how to build this temple for our honey bees long ago. Yet everything flowers in its own time, so perhaps it's not too late?

Skye
Schull
Ireland

CHAPTER ONE

At the Entrance to the Hive

"If you were invited into another realm, would you go in?"
Brenda to Skye 1976

'Tis passing strange: how something as small as a bee can catch our attention so well, delight us so easily and concern us so deeply. Intuitively we sense a kinship with this creature apart from our usual human/insect relationship. Many of us become very fond of bees, fascinated by them, caught by them. It has always been said that bees choose their keepers, it's a kind of calling, a Ministry of Bees!

When it happens, you notice Bees everywhere ~ in books, movies and direct transmissions, they start to pervade your life. Then, one day you want a hive. Ah! the journey begins!

I was given my first hive by Sam Comfort in 2007. He came over one day with a couple of boxes, one regular square Langstroth hive and one small trough shaped top-bar hive. We placed them a few feet away from each other in a glade near the barn where I was living and off he went.

I took a weekend class with Chris Harp who had studied under the biodynamic beekeeper and farmer Gunther Hauk. I learned a whole lot about bees the first day and far too much about disease and chemicals on day two. Then I joined the local bee guild and learned a lot from old timers and 'newbees' alike. I asked a lot of questions and read a lot of books. More than anything though, I simply stood near those hives every day, wondering and waiting.

I was afraid of bees. I was afraid of getting stung, not once, but again and again. In my mind bees and wasps were still hooked together and I had been stung many times by wasps. Only once had I been stung by a bee and that was while I was in monastic training at Tassajara in the Carmel Valley of California. It was spring and we had just completed our 'rigorous winter training' and I had been given the job of head gardener for the summer. When I heard that someone was going to check the bee hive I asked to go along. I didn't even know there was a hive at the monastery, though I had been there for many months. The small group of us who went to check the hive had an air of being on a mission. Clearly this was a risky operation. The 'bee-keeper' (actually the carpenter) told us all to stand aways off and then just took the lid off the hive without any warning. As the bees darted out, he began batting them away! I was amazed and alarmed, then one bee zoomed right in on my alarm and stung the tip of my nose. Ouch! That was that! No more bees for me ~ 'til they came calling many years later.

Standing still, in the glade behind the barn, watching and wondering, I am waiting for the whole of me to settle down and 'become friendly' with these bees. I notice how easy it is to feel tender toward one or two little bees when they are busy at blossoms, but a very different sensation arises within as I approach the entrance to the hive.

Breakfast time!

I remember a long time ago an older woman kindly looked at me and asked: "If you were able to enter another world would you go in?" I knew I would want to but I was not sure if I could, if I would have enough courage. It felt like that when I went to Tassajara. Could I do this 'rigorous zen practice'? I had heard tales, had my own imaginings of course, and knew it would not be easy. I heard there was no escape. That was tricky. I always liked to have an escape.

At the beginning of temple training the new monks sit together all day long, with breaks only after meals for half an hour or so. Long, long days from 4am to 9pm, just coming down to rest, leaving the busy world behind, becoming friendly with the monastery sounds and rhythms, adjusting to the food, the simplicity and most of all the silence. We sat like this for five days. It was wonderful. I found myself becoming more peaceful, my breath becoming steady and gratitude arising in a genuine way. I felt I had come home.

Tangaryo means 'waiting at the gate' and is the traditional transition for new members of the community to settle in and for the older members to get used to them, whilst not yet engaging with them. That comes next. For me this was the more difficult transition, the merging with the whole community.

When we chanted together it was glorious! Yet I found it a little intimidating interacting with so many monks and getting to know them all, without actually talking to anyone. It was all in our body language, how we bowed as we passed each other, how we served soup or rang a bell. These were the ways we got to know each other, the ways we expressed ourselves. Being uniform in dress and habit, our individuality stuck out.

Tassajara zendo

If you were looking into the temple from the outside though, you would not see that individuality. You would see uniformity. Lots of black-robed monks, male and female, moving slowly around in a deliberate way, with one brown-robed monk at the center of it all. Everything humming along nicely. Just like a bee hive!

I found I could enter the world of monastic living and thrive there. I was able to become friendly enough, to fit in, to take my place and contribute enough, that our relationship felt balanced.

How was I going to come into that same balance with these bees? There were so many of them! Those were just the ones coming in and out across the threshold. Inside are many, many more: thousands of bees, maybe 30,000 in the early spring and up to 60,000 in summer! That is a lot of bees and my subliminal nervous system understood that. I worked hard to keep my mind still and to become present to the presence of Bee. Meditation helps, quieting the mind helps, coming into the heart is essential.

At the monastery every morning we chanted a sutra, a teaching of Lord Buddha, called The Heart Sutra. It is a short concise version of the basic philosophy of Buddhism and, as such, is dense and intense. As we chant together, eat together, meditate together, ring bells and sound drums, moving in our slow thoughtful ways, the monastic community acts as a cohesive whole, a single being, maintaining the disciplines and habits of its lineage, century after century, not dependent on individuality but on cohesion from within. Within a monastery this cohesion has a different scent, a different flavor, as each practice period of a hundred days will have its own quality, dependent upon the nature of the presiding abbot. The bells will be rung in the same rhythm at the same time, the chants and ceremonies will not change, yet the practice period will not ever be the same, feel the same, as new abbots lead the community through deep winter.

Within the hive of the Honey Bee, it is the Queen who presides.

Queen Bee with her maidens

'Great Bee' she is known as, by many nations. The archetype of Bee, the matrix or essence of Bee, is palpable within the hive. Coming closer, even taking a seat close enough to hear the internal hum and smell the honey, I began to get a sense that all this activity, all these little moving parts are actually one being. I had read about and understood the concept of a super-organism, such as coral, some fungi, and termites. Yet I did not realize, until I spent some time with them, that honey bees also live not as individuals, but as separate moving parts of one single organism, a colony of bees. This colony of bees is one creature, one whole being, a complex and beautiful creation whose nucleus is the Queen. She is Great Bee manifest, a perfect embodiment of an extra-ordinary archetype.

Everybody wants to see the Queen!
Look carefully and you will see quite a few things: how big she is and yet how hard she is to see. Always surrounded by her handmaidens, always moving, never resting, it's hard to see the Queen!

However, you will always know if she is at home. Without her there is no actual cohesion to the colony, no unifying influence. Nothing gets done and the colony has no chance of survival. If the Queen dies and is not replaced with a new one, the remaining bees will gradually die. If you see a hive get listless and slow down with fewer bees coming and going, more robber bees getting in unchallenged, then you have probably lost your Queen.

The easiest way to lose a Queen is through careless or unfortunate handling of the comb by the beekeeper, though sometimes she will fail. Many commercially-bred queens do not live more than a year.

In an emergency the bees themselves will manage to create a new Queen. This is an incredible process that we will explore later when we enter the world of Worker bees. Suffice it to say that the colony will do whatever it can to produce a Queen and to take care of her at all costs ~ without her they cannot stay tethered.

The colony as a whole, this single organism, is composed of one Queen, a few hundred Drones (the boys), and many thousands of Worker bees (the girls) who, yes, do all the work except lay eggs, which is what the Queen does. The boys, we are told, simply wait around as potential suitors. More about that shortly.

7

What I find so fascinating is to contemplate some of the curious things about these bees. Queen Bee is, obviously, fertile. Drones are, also obviously, fertile. Workers are sterile though. Only the Queen mates and lays eggs and she has the ability to lay sterile or fertile eggs. As with all cases of parthenogenesis, sterile eggs give birth to male offspring. In a Bee hive the Queen will lay an infertile, or sterile egg in a cell built to nurse a Drone. She will lay a fertile egg in a cell built to nurse a Worker. To maintain her hive a Queen has to have mated, otherwise she can only lay sterile eggs which only produce Drones and they don't gather nectar or pollen or clean house, or even know how to feed themselves. If you notice a huge number of Drones or a lot of drone comb in your hive, you probably have a sterile Queen.

Worker bees build all their comb accordingly, making slightly bigger hexagonal cells for boys than for girls. If the Queen has mated, she can 'choose' to lay either a fertile or a sterile egg and the size of the comb cell she is laying the egg in will prompt that 'choice'. Thus the whole colony contributes to that decision.

Here we see the balance of opposites in play. A sterile egg gives rise to a fertile (boy) bee. A fertile egg gives rise to a sterile (girl) bee. In the case of the Queen however, a fertile egg gives rise to a fertile female (no 'girl' here)! That Queen is sure interesting! The whole system has a strange elegance, a mysterious nature. It has a sense of yin/yang balance, yet is dominated by the feminine.

When at the entrance, long before I opened the hive, I was getting a sense of all this, the moving beauty of it all. This allowed me to settle down and become friendly with the bees. They certainly had my respect. The question was, did I have theirs?

I wasn't sure. I *was* sure that I had to open the hive though. It was cold and the cluster going into winter was small with their honey larders probably not enough to get them through. I was working now with the top-bar hive, the one I felt most friendly with. In the Langstroth square box-hive the bees were too busy and driven for me. The bees (same lineage) in the top-bar hive went about things with a much more steady, steady pace and seemed to have a more natural sense of rhythm, shifting gears with the weather and not going out in the rain!

Both Sam and Chris thought this colony would die of cold over the winter. It was one of the familiar deep snow winters of upstate New York and the hive was low to the ground, with a simple thin cover and a bag of leaves thrown on top of that. I went to them as often as I could slog through the snow, just to let them know I was still around. Why? I don't know, but I had to go and visit, so I did. I listened quietly, as when snow fell and stillness was pervaded with fresh silence.

Gradually I felt I heard some sort of distress. The colony was running out of food. It was February and there were two more months before the bees could reliably find food or even leave the hive. Opening the hive would lower the internal temperature just when they needed most warmth. Not feeding them was not an option in my mind. I had no veil, no hat, no gloves, no idea of what I was doing, total beginners mind ~ but I did know I had to open that hive and that I needed Her Majesty's permission.

I waited three days before I felt that permission granted in some small way. This permission had a sense of yielding to it, with undertones of caution. I had been told to pour cane sugar into the hive near the cluster so they could reach something. Bees can't digest liquid in winter because their guts are not up to heat, they have lowered their body temperature to conserve energy and only caster sugar really helps them then. I stood at the entrance, breathing steady and slow. I took the lid off the hive and eased a bar from its propolis glue to lift it up. I was deeply focused in my heart center and repeating "It's only love" to myself. Swiftly a large number of bees flew straight up in front of my face ~ heart fluttered, mind stayed steady. I said out loud, "It's only love; it's only love", chanting my mantra to these bees, "It's only love" ~ and they all hovered a moment and then simply dropped back down into their nest. I poured in some sugar, replaced the bar and put the lid back on, amazed! They made it through that winter.

Since then I have never worn a veil or gloves, but I am slow and careful with these wild ones, these lovely honey bees.

To get close to beauty, sometimes you just have to take a risk.

Mid winter: hibernation…

The temptation to leave the temple too soon, to leave before the practice period is over, this temptation gained momentum as the monastery schedule started to sink into my bones. It is very cold in here sitting, sitting still, sitting long.
Black-robed silence covers our internal clamorings.
The abbess swishes her robe just a tiny bit extra.
Nothing extra here.
Almond tree blossoms improbably early, tempting escape again. Again I reach the zendo door and look out toward the garden yearning to simply weed, yet one foot steps in front of the other, no pushing, no pulling of body or mind, as I turn instead, again, to wall gazing.
I become aware of roots growing under me, a shoot starting to climb up my spine, I turn my awareness down to roots, it is too soon for leaves.
Down, down into the black silence ~ full of sounds without voice ~ we dive, each of us, in our own ways now, this mid-winter. Sitting still, sitting long, we reach further yet with our deepening roots until we touch a roaring silence, that utterly inexpressible place of loneliness and separation, that place where we believe we are all alone, one little seed all alone.
Then, right there, we too are touched ~ by our own heart/mind's searching for wholeness. A new sense, a new reference point, a new perception is born.
Suddenly, we belong.
Everything changes. We turn toward spring, still sitting, still gazing, no rushing, no running allowed in this monastery.

In the hive, in winter, bees are clustering around their Queen keeping her warm and fed while they all lower body temperature and minimize movement for the duration of this cold season. When a clear and sunny day above 45 degrees comes along, they go out on cleansing flights, relieving themselves, since they will never soil their nest. Then they go back into cluster quickly, before they lose too much heat ~ and they wait.

Day after day, night after night ~ steady, steady…

Hive in Winter

Oddly enough I had to leave the monastery during winter practice, an unheard of event for a new monk. I had to go to court. I was driven out of the wilderness to our gate house where I had parked my motorbike. It wouldn't start after so long in such cold. I had to travel to the city by bus. It was a remarkable experience. Most of all I recall the visceral sensation of standing still, quite still, surrounded by the anxious activity that distinguishes some of the old Greyhound bus stations. The people were poor and wore hardship, moving within a soup of suffering that I knew but did not make sense to me. I was in another world and thought it prudent to stay there whilst out on this brief cleansing flight. I don't even remember the passage home, it was so swift and direct. Business done, back to the cluster of robes.

I had already changed. This is what made sense to me now: this sitting, sitting still, sitting together, in a silence punctuated only by temple sounds, our collective chanting and the guiding words of a daily teaching from the abbess.

Waiting at the entrance for so long, opening the hive and taking that risk, listening to Queen Bee for her silent consent: all this changed me again.

These bees and I had become friendly enough.

They required me to step back, to calm my mind and let it rest in my heart. From there I breathed through fear, to a space where I could hear.

It's only love.

CHAPTER TWO

Inside the Hive

*Bees keep their brood in a climate whose
temperature is the same as ours.*

Although we say that the Queen is the nucleus of the hive, this is both true and yet not quite right. A colony can support and be held together by a succession of Queens. Over time a healthy colony will swarm and a new Queen will emerge to continue honeycomb life. Essentially a successful colony ever replaces itself and could be seen as immortal. There is no natural reason for a Honey Bee colony to just die. Naturally, they just tend to keep going, like monasteries.

The natural life cycle of a Queen is 8 years

The natural life cycle of a Worker is 9 weeks

The natural life cycle of a Drone is up to 4 months

Now a Queen Bee is unlikely to stay with her first colony for her whole life. Once her brood is large enough, when the pantries are full, the comb bursting with new bees and honey, right then she will simply up and leave them all to it, while she flies off with up to half her older kids to start all over again. That, to me, is radical generosity and radical trust! Usually mom sweeps the kids out of the house to fend for themselves. Not our Honey Bees. They set it all up, get it all humming along nicely and, just when the time is right, off goes the Queen with her adventurous band.

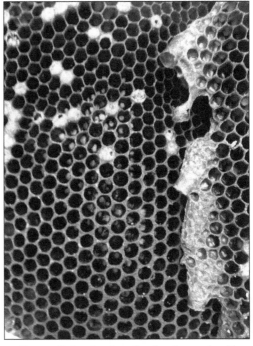

Queen cells hanging from the edge of a comb, with grubs in cells nearby to the right and capped brood, still forming bees, above to the left.

The signs of swarming are subtle, the swarming itself is always sudden, yet there have been weeks of preparation. Within the hive workers build a number of queen cells, elongated pendulous sacs unlike any other cell. They are usually built on the edge of the curve of honeycomb, sometimes one above the other.

Queen lays an egg in each, giving rise to her own dynastic legacy, leaving it for them to sort out who reigns after she has gone. The workers who stay with the hive tend it more slowly, some drones wander.

In the scheme of monastic life I tend toward drone activity. I like to be away from buildings, in the gardens, tending the grounds. I feel confined within the walls of kitchen or office and don't have the worker bee mind of simply doing what is in front of me. I like to wander and fortunately my teachers have seen that this is best for me. By 1994 I was the gardener for a Tibetan Buddhist retreat center in Northern California. I was in the gardens with my trusty wheelbarrow walking along the path one day, when another monkey monk ran up and said, "Come and offer a katak, Rinpoche is leaving!" Leaving? I knew, but did not want to know, and was secretly hoping to miss it so that I did not have to see him go. I had seen my elders leave too many times I thought, but there I was, drone to the end, with perfect timing: here was his car. I had a silk offering scarf tucked into my shirt pocket and I bent to offer it to a holy Tibetan man who had seen my wild side and not judged it at all, but allowed it to roam. There is a Zen saying: if you want to tame a sheep, give it the whole field. He had done that for me, given me the whole range to tend, so when it came time to be confined in the shrine room or serve in the dining room I did not chafe so much.

Rinpoche was swarming. He was our Queen and he was leaving us, heading to Brazil! Half the senior students went with him, mostly his close entourage. During the transition of his leaving it was easy to feel the glue of the retreat center coming undone. Our tight community of that glorious summer started to shift. Just when things were humming along, just when the mandala of sand felt complete, it was all swept away and off he went.

Until the new Queen is hatched and then mated, the hive is now weak, her pheromones are not pervading or embracing it. We felt the same, that Rinpoche's blessings were not holding us so close. Those of us who were new to the community and did not have the depth of practice, quickly fell into this sense of abandonment and slowly left. Drones get lost sometimes…quite lost without a Queen.

Before she leaves the hive, fertile eggs are laid in those special cells and then our Queen stops producing any more. Her handmaidens run her around the honeycomb tracks so that she loses enough weight to be able to take flight again. Meanwhile others are tending the new queen grubs, feeding them exclusively with royal jelly from the day they emerge from those pivotal eggs.

In a few days these grubs will be ready to transform and the cell will be capped. Then the hive is ready to split. The energy of the abdicating queen is waning in the hive and, by some esoteric manner probably guided by Drones, decisions have been made as to which little bee stays and which leaves. Drones determine timing in the hive and when all is perfectly poised they give the signal to swarm.

This is the true reproductive act of a colony much like a single cell division. The one organism that is a bee colony splits into two. The laying of eggs in the brood chambers, the production of little bees, is not so much about reproduction as it is about cell replacement. We could think perhaps that the girl bees, the Workers, are like our blood cells continually being replaced. Drones are akin to our nervous system. Queen rules through the glands.

Standing close to my hives I noticed that the bees always went back to the 'right' one. This glandular signature of Queen Bee is very strong, a chemical scent that pervades everything in the hive ~ all the comb, all the wax on every bee's body, the whole is permeated by her unique personal odor. Those girls know who they belong to and they know who does and does not belong.

At the entrance every day, except when they were very, very busy, I saw a few bees with their butts up in the air like a stink beetle. It seems they do stink a bit themselves, these guard bees, and you can see them fanning the odor from tiny glands, marking the threshold and defending their Queen! Should a strange bee come along they will attack and repel it. If need be they will kill by stinging but that is a last resort. Unlike a wasp, a honey bee dies when it stings. The stinger is barbed and does not disconnect. It pulls the bee apart. She will fly off for a moment, lose balance and drop dead. The whole colony gives up some individuals to defend the whole. We are very familiar with that scenario. We send out our forces, bees send out their girls. Drones can't sting, nature made sure of that. They have other work to do!

Drones are the boys on the block and they tend to have a very bad reputation. People see them hanging out in gangs doing nothing, coming home to get fed and heading back out again. Waiting. Waiting for a single moment of eye-popping death-inducing sex.

Really? Hail to the Mighty Drone!

There is so much more to these lads than mere 'nuptial arrangements'. They are magnificent creatures! Physically they are larger than the girls with a bulbous bod and huge eyes. Huge: 600 hexagonal lenses in each eye! Imagine that …imagine that coming at you, reflecting so much light (as hexagons do ~ our road signs are composed of them). Brilliant lads these Drones! All suited up and bristling. They even have hair growing out of their eyes. They are all a-quiver.

Beyond sex ~ and yes there is life beyond sex ~ what is all this dazzling equipment for? A bee hive is so very efficient and orderly, how could these lads be as utterly useless in it as most people think? Of course, they are not. Their very presence exudes all sorts of information.

Drones are the barometers of the hive. They inform the hive of incoming weather. Generally their hangouts are a few hundred feet up in the air, far above trees and forage. Drones from different hives congregate and then go back home to be fed.

When you sit at your hive watching and noticing you will see Drones take off differently from Worker foragers. Drones lazily lift off as if that bulbous bod fills with warm air and up he goes! When returning they don't generally land neatly but tend to tumble back as if slightly disoriented from the altitude shift.

Then they enter the hive bristling with information about immanent weather: wind, temperature, air pressure, moisture and all that stuff, which they impart to the hive through their presence in it ~ just as you can tell what is going on outside when your 17 year old tumbles in the door and heads to the fridge. Frequency, vibration, chemical coding, awareness, call it what you will, the hive is informed by its

Drones about the larger ecosystem in which it lives. Drones are the antennae, the weathermen of the hive.

The reach of the 'mind' of the hive, through the Drones in altitude and the Workers in distance, is extraordinary. Workers will fly up to three miles from home for forage and Drones fly high above. The connective tissue, the signature chemistry of their Queen maintains their link to the home comb. Perceiving the whole as one we are awed by the reach of this beautiful creature.

Without a balance of Drones, the hive is out of sync with its outer micro-climate, unaware of storms coming in, no longer adjusting to nectar flow and unable to regulate the brood chamber accordingly.

Within the hive it seems likely that Drones cast a lot of light, having such reflective enormous eyes. They wander around, seemingly aimlessly, looking for a Worker bee to feed them since they can't feed themselves. Yet that is not all they are doing. They also function as a sort of crew boss, indicating what work needs to be done in the hive, when bees need to shift into other jobs ~ all the transitional aspects within the hive. It is well known that when the Sun is thirty degrees past its zenith (around 3pm in summer), Drones will conduct an orientation flight for new forager bees who will start to collect nectar and pollen the next day. In this flight they are introduced to the outside of the hive, so that later they will be able to find their way back safely.

When we look at all these ways of behaving and consider their place in the whole system of the bee hive ~ the process of the hive as a single being ~ we can say with some confidence that Drones are responsible for Timing. They bring in the information that prompts the colony to shift gears according to the barometric pressures of the day. Drones probably prompt swarming and yes ~ their ultimate offering is essential on the day of the nuptial flight! They die in coitus.

Ah! the Mighty Drone!

Then there are all those girls! These Worker bees are far less glamorous than their matinee idol/idle brothers, yet they are the ones we know. It's the girls we see out upon the flowers and it's the girls coming home with bags packed with pollen, tummies filled with nectar and tongues filled with water for the rest of the hive. These girls do everything, they are so amazing. The very first thing they do when they crawl out of their birth cell is turn right around and make it all nice and clean for its next job, be that for honey storage or brood chamber. Then it's off to work. This bee will not leave the hive for three weeks. She will go through a series of jobs according to the needs of the hive at any moment and according to her age and innate abilities. All bees are a little different actually, no two are totally alike it seems. All talents are useful in the hive.

At first the young bee does clean up duties. Bees are meticulous and keep everything swept out daily, removing bits of wax dropped when the cap of a cell gets broken open as a new bee emerges. Sometimes foreign objects appear and have to be dragged out to the entrance and cast over the edge. If something gets in and is too large for them to handle, they will encase it in propolis to ensure it does not cause disease within the hive. Bees do not tolerate invasive organisms lightly.

Since we are talking about One Bee we can understand how this use of propolis is imperative to the health of the hive. No one, apparently individual, bee has her own immune system, just as no one aspect of your body has its own. Our immune system is internal, within our body as a whole. We have a blood-brain barrier too, which means that disturbances within the organs, bones and tissue are served by the blood, so we look there for diagnosis of the body. To look for disturbances of the brain and neurological system though we must take a different view, because that information will not cross over the barrier into the blood system. So we have created MRI's and other clever tools to see things with from different perspectives. All mammals have this separation of immune functions. The immunity of our neurology is the glandular system, the pineal gland leading the way, the adrenals triggering alarm. The chemistry released by the glandular system will flood the neurological, digestive and lymphatic pathways and end up getting flushed through the body, pouring out in urine, sweat and tears. If that process gets interrupted, disease will set in. The system will have become clogged.

The biology of little 'individual' bee seems to be quite fluid. They have lots of glands containing ingredients for all stages of honey production. They have glands in their heads from which the Queen's attendants will produce the famed royal jelly with which to feed Her Majesty. The gut of a healthy bee has innumerable bacteria and microbes that do all sorts of amazing things beyond my comprehension. There isn't much solid about a bee, really. The bones are external, being the wax comb of the hive, the intestines are dedicated to the mystery of transformation, making honey out of flower juice. There must be lots of air channels to help them fly, so far, so long, since they don't have feathers and their wings are tiny. They look solid but things are not what they seem all the time. Bee, as a collective creature, does not need to place a tiny immune system in every moving part ~ it simply surrounds itself with that protection at home. Foragers and Drones leave that protection daily.

Bees seal their hive with propolis. This is a gummy substance gleaned from the buds of trees and some barks which the girls will gather, masticate and transform with their own glandular juices to become the so-called glue of the hive. Every hanging bar of comb is held in place and every crack is blocked with propolis, which is anti-bacterial, anti-fungal and anti-viral in its properties.

Gathering this propolis is work for older bees though, and ours is yet young. She is working her way through the basic chores around the hive body and on the honeycomb itself. There she will transport food perhaps, feed a Drone upon demand, repair honeycomb, fan her wings as needed for heating or cooling the internal temperature ~ ever maintaining the climate and cleanliness of the hive. Brood rearing; tending the Queen; guarding the hive; delivering food; receiving nectar from forager bees and taking it into the hive when the flow is on (so they don't lose time gathering); fanning the comb to maintain airflow and temperature so the comb doesn't melt or get brittle; heating empty cells in the brood chamber so the babies nearby are warm enough; building new comb as the hive expands ~ all these and probably more, are the basic jobs that the girls do. There is a mild busyness in a thriving hive, not a frantic pace at all, but a steady constant movement of little bodies tending to every detail as they roam around the hanging gardens of brood and honey.

Making honey out of nectar is a somewhat metaphysical process whereby the bee will mix the nectar within her own glandular system and gut, within which are many bacteria that have to do with both digestion and fermentation. Somehow, out of all that mixing and creating, the golden medicine is made and stored inside a cell of wax comb.

The girls make the comb, too, of course. This time they don't have to go out for any supplies at all. They simply sweat the wax platelets out of their little flanks, chew on that, and form hexagonal cells that fit together and are plumb-lined perfectly (any tilt would spill the larder). To do this they hold on to the bar, or branch, all in a line hanging on with their forelegs, and then another group holds onto their back legs, and then others hold onto theirs, until a chain of bees hangs down plumbing the line for the new comb. Then they sweat it out and build it together, starting at each end sometimes and meeting in the middle without any squishing of geometry. Every comb is built up on both sides with the center point of one hexagonal cell providing the support base for the cell on the other side. Onto this exact axis an egg can be laid, sticking upright, perfectly supported by the incredible exactitude of the bees building brigade. Every cell of the whole comb is very slightly tilted upward so the contents stay put, though the whole garden of comb is perfectly hung in a catenary curve.

Perfect Geometry

Honeycomb ~ naturally

What happens to a colony of bees when they are not given space to create this comb, when they do not wax out? Does that clog up their systems?

In the rarest of cases a single Worker bee can make internal changes so great that she (who is sterile) can produce a fertile egg that will become the new Queen![1] The time lapse in the brood chamber, should this emergency arise, also requires many of the workers to reverse age, so that the tasks of the hive are maintained beyond their normal life span. They make internal shifts to bridge the gap. Their ability to do all that they do, appears to be based on the temperature in the brood chamber during gestation.

It is interesting that this temperature issue is such a big deal. If a grub stays even slightly too cold it will not produce a bee able to do all the work in the hive. Too hot and presumably it will cook. Especially at risk are the higher crafts of wax making and honey making. About four-fifths of the honey produced in a hive goes toward energy costs, running the hive at a high enough temperature to maintain continual brood activity, repel invaders, stash some more honey for later and keep everyone from overheating when the high summer comes.

What happens when honey stores are taken away by us? Doesn't that upset the internal balance of the hive? Is there a balance of 'enough' rather than 'more' that we could reach for here?

It takes a lot to keep things going in there! All of this is done by the girls: our sterile, born of fertile eggs, girls. There is a legendary self-lessness about these bees. Within the hive the focus of sexuality is located in the Queen. There can only be one Queen and so there is no need for any other fertile female. It is as if the gender issue becomes moot but for that fascinating yin/yang juxtaposition, which presents through the sterility of the girls in particular. "Work is Love" is the motto of honey bees, adopted by many as example and guide.

These girls work, and the hum of their work, the magic of honey, the wonder of all the activity in the hive is theirs. For three weeks they will live on the comb in the hive. Then, all being well, they will start to use their wings, not just for fanning and short cleansing flights, but now for long-distance foraging, all day long. Drones will orient them to the outside world, making sure they have home-base imprinted in their little internal GPS systems. Next day they are off, Sun creatures now, seeking nectar, gathering pollen.

Out in the field the new foragers will be following directions given by scout bees who have been out early and figured out who's blooming right now. These are older girls, experienced. They come back to the hive and give the famous waggle dance, turning around and around, waggling their butt in a dance they repeat and repeat, 'til other bees start doing it with them, get it right and then off they all go…harvest time!

If the flow is on and heavy, even the guard bees will leave their post and head off to the flowering fields. Most flowers, especially fruit flowers, don't last long, though they are generous with their nectar while they do. Bee and Hummingbird both know to revisit each flower about twenty minutes later when she has had time to refill the cup. She of course keeps inviting them back to pick up pollen for her, which she can't deliver herself. Bees are happy to oblige and get to keep a hand-some load for their trouble. Pollen is the protein of the hive and essential for the rearing of brood. When mixed with honey it is called bee bread and this mix is used for the later stages of grub development.

What happens in the brood chamber when traps are used to scrape the pollen from the legs of bees as they enter the hive? Does the brood suffer? Are the new bees still strong and healthy?

This issue of the health of Workers is also connected to the health of Drones who mated with Queen who produced those girls. In other words, if Queen did not naturally mate many times during her nuptial flight with healthy Drones from other hives, as is usually the case, she would not have received enough diversity of sperm to ensure the fullest health of the gut and glands of her brood. When the sperm input is low, or artificially induced, the brood is weakened, especially in the guts of the girls. The transformative work of honey-making takes place in their guts. When these Workers are weak it is probably harder to maintain the high temperature required of the hive, so more honey would be needed, which means more work. Any hive with this subtle stress will probably not survive very long, unless the next Queen mates more successfully.

Staying wild strengthens.

CHAPTER THREE

Freya

It is not our bees that we must master, it is our own way of being with the wild we must master. Bees are wild through and through.

Freya was bound to go feral. She swarmed six weeks after I hived her. Six weeks! It takes three weeks to produce a new wave of bees. First the comb has to be built, then eggs laid. She must have been in full form upon arrival!

I picked her up at the post office who had called early to let me know she was humming there and, "No rush please," the post folk were enjoying her company! I paused for a while, yet soon had to run in and get her. Behind the post-lady was a pervasive humming, unmistakable and music to my ear. I must have been glowing with anticipation! Once in my hands I gently lifted the mesh front of the box close to my face as tiny ones moved away a little, scaling up their hum. No worries, it seemed that Queen was alive inside somewhere, deep in that mass of bees.

To start a hive you have to either catch a swarm; buy a baby hive, take it to your place and move all the comb into a bigger hive there; or you buy a package of bees. This is a completely arbitrary collection of bees, meaning the Workers will not be related to the Queen who is deliberately bred by 'beeks' (beekeepers) who do such things. Worker bees are vacuumed into the traveling box, a can of sugar syrup is hung into that space, perforated so bees drink from below. A Queen is suspended in a special cage into this three pound weight of bees and a lid slapped on quick, stapled down well. The post office will deliver. Quickly.

I consider myself lucky if there are any Drones aboard when the package arrives. Most important of all, you want to have a live Queen, one that the rest of the girls will eventually accept as their own. That is not a given.

I would say this is not a natural way to produce

Freya's first swarm

29

bees. Yet it is a random thing to catch a swarm and who knows what you might be catching! So to start a new hive I have decided to settle on this until some other option is created. I order a package of bees, usually in January or February, they will arrive in April and can be available through May in most places.

I was living on the California coast and about to hive these bees there in the fog belt. On the same day I drove over the ridge into the sunny Silicone Valley and hived a package of bees from the same bee farm, sister hives. Sophia's hive became known as Eden, after a special rose grown at Grandma's house. Mine came with the name Freya.

I put her whole traveling box into the body of her hive for a while to settle down. I wanted those bees to get over the shock of this false swarming and to attune to this Queen. I think it is a mistake to rush this process, to want to get them out of there as soon as you can. Let them stay, allow the cluster around their Queen time to generate swarm mind within them. This will knit them together, allowing her scent to pervade and embrace, to lead and, upon acceptance, serve ~ as all true leaders do. Later, when you *do* hive them, they will be more likely to stay together and accept your hive. By placing their traveling box into the body of their new hive they get adjusted to it all together.

I put them in their hive at evening, left them there for another day and then went back to let them out of the box and into the hive before sundown.

Freya was pissed, I could tell…she was turning around and around and what I had not known was that, in this case she had not been given attendants to travel with. She was alone in that cage and that is not good for a Queen. Previously I had only received packages where the Queen had four or five attendants with her, all suspended in a small cage within the box. The other bees cluster around her, as they would do naturally in a swarm. This time she was alone. I did not like that. Neither did she.

I could feel the difference between this Queen and Eden as my fingers carefully lifted her cage out of the box, trying not to let hundreds of bees fly out at the same time. You have to move slowly, being so careful not to hurt any one. Bees will get all over your hands and fingers, but will not sting at all unless you are careless; they have other issues right now. They need to build comb. Our Queen's single issue is to get out of her cage. In this case, being alone, she needed grooming and feeding immediately!

If you wait too long to hive your bees you will see them beginning to drop tiny platelets of wax as it sweats out of their flanks. Without comb there is no honey and no brood. There is no home. Bees do not drink nectar or eat pollen directly, they make it into honey and bee bread within the honeycomb cells and absolutely have to build that comb as soon as possible, right now!

I tie a string around the Queen cage and suspend it into the empty space of the hive body about four bars from the end. I already divided the length of the hive with a following board to only offer the bees about half the space to start with. I want them to make straight comb on the bars so I can lift them and see what is happening later on. I give them about eight or nine bars and block off the rest for a while, hang the Queen in the middle of that space and then tip the rest of the bees out of their box into the hive. Many of them simply pour out like water, others take a while and I usually make a ramp from the box to the hive entrance for the stragglers to use after the lid of the hive is on. They will go to their Queen.

One really important thing to not forget, as I almost did with Freya, is to take out the cork at the bottom of her little cage. Behind this is another small plug made of sugar candy which her girls will eat through in order to release their Queen, thus ensuring the connective tissue between them all. She should be out in three days. If I had known these Queens had no attendants I would have risked hiving them earlier, but in the end no harm was done, they both survived, Eden and Freya.

As far as we know (and we are pretty sure about this), Eden has not swarmed yet, now nine months later. This is a good sign, a strong and steady hive which we would expect to see swarm this coming spring rather than before.

Freya had other ideas. She swarmed at six weeks old. Amazing! Amazing and troubling too. I was not amused. "Really?" I said, when my friends who hosted her phoned with the news. "Are you sure that's our hive? I think it's too soon." Little did I know! Indeed, she had already, in six weeks, built enough comb, laid enough eggs, bred enough brood to create a rather large swarm that was now hanging in the bottle brush tree.

I wanted none of it! I was already long aggravated by this forced rearing of Queens (though I had no solutions yet) and decided not to catch that swarm, but to let her go feral to see how the bees left behind fared with what I hoped would be a new Queen shortly to arise.

My friends thought I was crazy, but Freya I did not pursue, in her first swarming nor in her second, which incredibly came three weeks after the first. Now I was getting worried. The girls were very gentle and, though busy, not really, really busy as one would expect in mid-summer. The first cultivated Queen had fled with half the bees. The second bee-bred Queen had left with yet more of the girls, so who was here to do the work now? To do the math always makes my head ache so I usually do it lying down. Now I am counting bee days instead of sheep!

Freya was hived May 10th. When I checked the hive after three days to remove the Queen cage and ensure she was out of it ~ she wasn't. I broke through the rest of the sugar candy and watched her scramble out of that trap and run straight into the hive. That was the 13th. If she started laying eggs right away, which would have been possible since her girls had already built three or four bars of comb, it then takes 21 days for new Worker bees to hatch. Queen Freya could have turned out a thousand to fifteen hundred eggs a day. So at the max, by six weeks she could have produced waves of new bees every day for three weeks ~ about thirty thousand bees or more. I had increased the size of the internal space of the hive every week by moving the divider or following board down, revealing more bars for them to use, so the comb build-ing could continue. Freya swarmed when the hive was two-thirds full, though not all the bars offered had been used yet. For a second swarm to happen three weeks later seemed to me to be a sign of weakness, of perhaps a Queen that was not viable, or an unusual agreement between two new Queens which I thought unlikely.

I had to open the hive to check. I had waited after the initial swarming, not wanting to interrupt the hive while a new Queen took over. I was slowly shocked by what I saw. It took some time to under-stand what I was looking at.

Bar after bar of full comb was covered in Drones who were moving very slowly if at all, as if stunned, presumably because no one was feeding them. Bar after bar of Drones, it was eerie, as if they knew something was wrong. Way further down in the original brood nest a few girls were still valiantly tending the bones of a sterile Queen.

I thought it unlikely this hive would survive. I did nothing to help it or intervene in any way after this inspection. I left the Drones where they were. The girls would show me what they could do.

All this time the hive is in another garden since folks near me were allergic (and afraid), so I do not see her every day but I drive by and check in often. Dee goes to the hive every day wishing to become a beek herself. After the swarm she was happy to find she could sit close to the entrance and not seem to bother her bees or get bothered by them. Sometime in August she called to let me know that she was getting annoyed, because those bees wouldn't let her get so close anymore. Then I knew Freya had recovered herself! A too placid hive is a weak one usually; one that defends itself has a strong Queen. Somehow those bees born of the first Queen had managed to stay alive through one sterile Queen's journey of three weeks, during which time no new workers were bred. Then, one of these older workers managed to go through those internal changes to produce a fertile egg in order to create a third new Queen.[2] She took sixteen days to hatch out and a couple more to figure out where she was, and then one or two more days for those nuptial flights, hopefully with other healthier Drones. Then, the girls had another three weeks of brood tending (not forgetting all the other chores inside and out) until a new wave of Worker bees hatched out at last. After that it still takes another three weeks for any of these new troops to be ready to go foraging. The girls that bridged the crisis must have lived about twice the normal life span of a little Worker bee.

I left that hive in situ through the winter rains to see how she fared. Early in the spring I received this message: "Please come and take them away, asap! They are too unfriendly!" Wonderful, I thought, she did great! I will get her as soon as I can.

I have to be very careful though, I lost my first Queen when moving her swarm. I didn't think it through all the way, I just wanted to get done. That mind doesn't work with bees. I find it easier to work out things like this when alone, when I can think. It takes a while and I enjoy the process of sorting things out, problem solving. The only way I have ever succeeded in this is when I solve the problem from some other point of view: one not about me. What needs to get done? That question always gets me out of the way. That's a good place to start!

When I was first given the job of head gardener at Tassajara I had no idea what I was doing, but also had no thought that I could not do it. I just needed to know what needed to be done. I clearly remember the head priest or director asking me in a slightly bewildered tone: "What makes you think you can do this?" (having no prior experience), and I simply said: "Ah, I'm English!" and that was that. I got the job! What a great job it was too, with so very much to do and to think about, so much to learn. I had to ask two people, "What needs to be done?" The first was the gardener who had been whisked into the fabled Tassajara kitchen for the summer as a guest cook. Only this made it possible for me to take on the gardens. I listened to her at the kitchen door (and interrupted a few sauces I'm sure), and she was kind and patient far more than I at that time. I was a bit overwhelmed as spring slowly revealed the extent of the gardens requiring attention, some of them not seeming to be feeling so good. I was given the overview, the budget and the requests: of food and herbs for the kitchen, flowers for the cabins and shrines, care of all grounds and gardens from end to end. When needing to stay quieter I especially loved to rake the abbot's garden. Eventually it looked like I knew what I was doing and all was growing well and looking lovely.

I was treated to a sweeping tour of the gardens by the renowned Wendy Johnson, who had created this garden from canyon bedrock years ago. She was visiting for a family break and Peter, her husband, was guarding her time away from them fiercely. I pleaded for half an hour. That's all it took. Moving as a force of nature, Wendy took me bed by bed, telling me how far to cut back and what to plant. No time to write a note, just focus, listen, absorb. When instructed to cut back a perennial herb "down to the ground," I softly enquired, "Shouldn't I leave a little for it to start with?" This elicited a slow, deliberate and withering gaze, accompanied by the equally slow and withering, "How far down?" "Down to the ground," I said humbly. I had found a teacher!

Highly motivated to tend these gardens well, I realized that I had no idea how to organize my time around all this. What did the garden need? Well, I had a lot of information about that. When should it get done was an additional dimension.

34

I sat in the gardener's shed for three days without pulling any weeds or cutting anything at all down to the ground. I pored over my notes, the biodynamic calendar, the monastery calendar, all the factors of time that had to somehow come together to let me see the patterns that the garden would probably like me to sync with. I figured out which beds to dig when; which seeds to sow when, all to do with the lunar and stellar patterns that inform our biography. Then I was ready. I knew it was useless for me to just pick up my trowel and do what was in front of me. I would get lost in the details and never tend the whole. I had to lift up to see the whole system that was Tassajara at that time, in that summer of 1990, and tend to the parts only in relation to that whole.

The author at Tassajara, 1990

I too was merely a part of the monastery of course, more transient than the stones I was asked to sweep when I first arrived: no less valued, no more.

This intrinsic and very palpable sense of place and purpose was familiar to me through my years in theatre. There too we are all exquisitely invaluable and un-equal. I worked at the sound console for some big and small musicals and, because I handed out the mics, I got to move everywhere in the theatre, in the hive. It seems I have ever been a Drone! Always popping out to check on weather and audience, al-ways walking around checking speakers and mics backstage and in the orchestra pit.

To run live sound you need to know all that is going on: the weather determines what kind of coats the audience is wearing and their mood. Cold and crisp is great, though listen out for sharpness in the sound. Cold and damp is tough, especially if all those coats come into the auditorium, soaking up the crispness you need. The whole show, lights ~ sound ~ action, is related to what the audience brings to the theatre from the outside. The work of the technicians is to adjust accordingly so the show is presented just so, no matter what the weather or mood. Yet the company must meet that weather, that mood and not just perform in a vacuum. When everyone gets it just right and the whole syncs up (company, theatre, audience, weather and mood), then we perform the most memorable of shows.

At the sound console

When the final curtain falls and the auditorium resounds with real applause, no matter what part you played ~ dresser, musician, stage hand, chorus or star ~ everyone is applauded. It's true that most of the 'Workers' simply go right on about their business quite unmoved, yet the Drones amongst us reflect it right back to our star, the Queen. She always gets a lot of attention!

36

Clearly it is time to talk about the Queen!
The Drones in the bee hive have a hidden way of dazzling by reflection, the Workers are utterly devoted ~ yet that Queen is sure something else! Here's a few factoids to start with:

It only takes sixteen days from egg to fully hatched Queen: five days less than a Worker and up to nine days less than a Drone. She can out-live them all, by years. A Queen cell is different from other cells and is constructed only when needed. It hangs down like a sack and this bee grows upside down, emerging from the bottom of the elongated cell. She is the only bee that can sting and sting again and she will do that only when fighting another Queen. Otherwise her girls will take care of things. Usually the colony will build a small number of Queen cells for obvious backup reasons. The first one out gets to sting first! She will go to the other Queen cells, rip off the cap and sting her potential usurper to death. Two Queens fighting in a hive make piping sounds not heard at any other time. The fight ends when only one Queen is left alive.

Once the royal line is thus clarified the new Queen must mate. Apart from this famous nuptial flight she never leaves the hive unless and until she swarms. She is raised as a grub and fed all her adult life with only Royal Jelly, an intense and pure food produced for her by her girls. She does not feed herself. She does not groom herself. She lays eggs, hundreds of them a day, endlessly producing waves of new bees to keep the system going. At the height of honey season she will lay about 1500 eggs a day, moving in a spiraling slow dance surrounded by handmaidens who groom and feed her.

Those are just basic facts. These are thoughts to ponder…

No bees pee or poop inside the hive, they are fastidiously clean.[3] The Queen never leaves. Royal Jelly has to be a most perfect food! No waste! The organism of the Queen Bee seems to me to be so perfectly balanced. She takes in this pure food, produces her own weight in eggs every day and never eliminates waste. I find that amazing, what a perfectly beautiful expression of life force. No other bee gets fed this Royal Jelly. Queen bees that are falsely raised by people don't always get it right away and this affects the life force of the resulting Queen. She probably won't live so long. A year or two or even three is considered good. Staying strong and wild though, she could live much longer, swarming year after year until she can no longer produce enough brood, then the colony will replace her. She will lay an egg into a specially built Queen cell, giving birth to the one who will take her place.

This is the natural cycle of a colony of bees, ever replacing, ever continuing, ever engaged in the mystery of creation.

A Queen swarms, taking up to half her colony with her. To prepare, Drones set the timing as Queen slows down her laying. New Queen cells are built and, just before she stops, eggs are deposited within. Then the girls race their Queen around the comb so she can lose weight! She cannot fly when producing eggs, she is too heavy. Her productive system gets shut down for a while and she slims down while the girls feed heavily so they have full tummies before the radical departure. Swarming out of the hive, bees move like water, flowing out together, pouring out of the hive and taking flight ~ around and around in spirals they go, creating a funnel of bees that moves up and away seeking a nearby hang out, a tree, a shrub, a lamp post. All bees gather around their Queen. Their whole attention is only on protecting her and finding a new nest site.

The sound of swarming is glorious and loud and powerful, thousands of bees are jazzed and full of purpose. It is a wonderful time to get close to them because they are not interested in you at all. They have no hive to defend, they are mid-adventure and cannot afford to combat. It is extra-ordinary to walk amongst swarming bees, to listen and watch as they flurry around you clustering around their Queen wherever she may decide to land. If you, human, are lucky she will land low enough for you to touch, to stroke her cluster, to feel the moving warmth of the colony in a way we cannot do within the hive. If you are fortunate enough to have a hive nearby and ready when a swarm occurs you can even slowly, gently, take those bees in your hands and carry them over to their new home.

Most folks are not going to do that though, but you could. It takes a meditative mind or a quiet mind to do this, a mind that is secure in the heart center, not in the head. This bringing the activity of mind down allows it both to rest and to see this whole we are talking about. To embrace the whole we have to be centered.

Our center is in our chest, not our head, not our pelvis. When we get used to being there we can both relate to wildness more easily and take our place within the whole where we meet. When we move from here, this handling of bees is not invasive or threatening, but supportive and kind. It's only love.

Usually you take your hive or some kind of interim container (a bucket or a box) and bring it up under the swarm. Then by sharply bouncing the branch they are hanging from you can catch them as they drop down. Lots of bees will take flight of course, but no worries, they are not interested in stinging right now, they need a home. The most important issue is that you get the Queen in the hive, then every one in flight or out scouting will join her when they are ready. You can tell right away if you have the Queen because some bees will immediately take up guard duty and stick up their butts at the entrance. That's a good sign. Time to put the lid on, leave it all where it is 'til twilight at least, so all the bees get home, and hope you have a good healthy swarm that will accept your hive offering.

Bees are somewhat fussy. They won't just accept any old box to set up their intricate home. Most of all they need a dry, clean, winter-proof space. Summer they can deal with, winter is hard on them. The scout bees will leave the swarm cluster to seek the right shelter and many of them may come back to the group with options. All decisions are made by consensus it seems and flights will go back and forth visiting those options 'til all agree and off they go again. Catching a swarm interrupts this process of course and offers them a particular place convenient to the beekeeper. It is up to them if they agree to stay. They might, and they might not. As long as it is tight against the rain, clean and spacious enough they will probably stay. It's risky staying outside overnight for bees. They need to find a new place within a very few days before they get really hungry. They can feed the Queen, but there is no honey for them until they build a new home.

As soon as they move into the new space great activity begins. Comb has to be plumb-lined, sweated out and built. Nectar and pollen must start coming in as soon as possible and that can't happen 'til there is somewhere to store it. Queen needs to gear up to her egg laying olympics and needs brood cells to lay in. These are very busy days. Drones are out and about getting all that local gossip about wind shear and rain clouds. Scouts are locating new fields of possibility, bringing in a variety of pollen and nectar, waggling away and getting food coming in. Gradually over a week or two whole bars of comb are created, filled with food or brood and kept under tight climate control.

Within one lunar cycle fresh baby bees will be hatching by the hundreds every day, ready to take the place of those now long exhausted.

In the hive great productivity ~ our Queen is laying well

In the hive great activity, our girls are maintaining

All systems steady steady

Coming into the hive vast quantities

Of flower juices and protein bars

Out on the lam, above it all

Drones are checking the weather

This is Great Bee in action

This is One Bee

CHAPTER FOUR

Listening

Until children, inside and out, are heard, are listened to,
we cannot come into wholeness.

One Bee: One Bee-ing ~ it's fun how we can say that in English, though of course other languages have their own words for Bee. In Greek it is *Melissa*, Meli sometimes. The Melissae had oracular powers we are told, a priestess lineage of an ancient Temple of the Honey Bee. They listened to Great Bee.

Sophia calls her hive Eden, as you know, and one day we were opening up the hive with some of her young friends helping, and I accidentally squished a bee as I was replacing a bar down the far end of the hive. We all heard the whole colony moan a little, far away from that one little bee. We all, in that sound, understood that it was the same as for us: when we squish our finger, our whole body moans, not just our finger. Then we knew Eden was one Great Bee; we had heard her.

This listening to your bees is really amazing. I was even given a stethoscope so I could listen to my hive in winter! Most of the time though you can just put your ear against the back of the hive and listen in to the gentle hum of thriving honeycomb life. After hiving a new packaged 'swarm' in the Hudson area a few years ago, I went to listen in and heard a high pitched whine. Right away I knew their Queen was in trouble and for some reason the girls couldn't get her out. The very moment she was released to them, the pitch and intensity of sound lowered throughout the hive. One Bee speaks clearly if you listen. You can listen at the hive, you can listen at the temple, you just have to get still inside.

It is said that you must tell your bees what is going on in your life, with your family and most especially to tell them of any deaths, or if you are going away. I have heard this from generations back and read of it in many odd places. One story spoke of provoking swarms if there was not enough personal integrity, not enough conversation, between hive and beekeeper. Another story spoke of bees heading out when arguments arise. It seems that there is a strange and wondrous connection between this hard-to-grasp singularity of Great Bee and our own awareness of other hard-to-grasp Singularities!

Ancient lore of many peoples have stories or customs around Bees and Honey. Honey was never to be taken to the market place. It was considered too sacred, revered as medicine and as an offering to royalty or temple. The mystical process of making this honey from the nectar of flowers was considered close to Divine. In fact some traditions say that God speaks to only one of His Earthly creatures directly, and that is Honey Bee. Listening to Bee has always been thought a good idea.

Our willingness to listen to Honey Bee may have a link to our ancient intuition that Bee Knows Something. That 'something' helps them be successful, productive and immortal. Since they are able and willing to produce and replace a Queen to benefit the whole, there is no sense actually that the colony, as a whole, naturally dies. It self-regenerates. It keeps going ~ why not? What would interrupt that? Big weather would for sure, but a colony in a strong dry location will be able to stay there indefinitely. There is a taste of the immortal here. We reach for that taste in the offering of pure honey. It can actually keep us alive for a while.

A brother of mine contracted some deadly disease at age four and was put into ICU with a diet of penicillin injections and pure comb honey for three months. Nothing else. He made it through. Honey, penicillin and prayer ~ a very powerful recipe for healing.

This combination of honey and prayer is well known throughout the world. Whatever local medicine may be dispensed is often mixed with honey, as a prayer is said, then the mix given to child or patient. Nowadays this has been replaced by 'a spoonful of sugar' and a command, which could not have the same effect at all. We are moving away from the Holy in so many ways, could it be that our Honey Bees are showing us the way back home?

Throughout the centuries we have always had this notion that we must listen to our bees, that they are messengers from the Divine. Even through the din of industry this intuition perseveres. This present notion, of our Bees telling us something, being the canary in our mine, follows on from that, of course. Have we really strayed so far, in so little time, from pure honey, from pure prayer?

We understand our Honey Bees are dying and that most folks are correctly busy proving this or that chemical product, used in our wider agricultural landscape, to be the problem. Banning these poisons is a good idea, yet it is not going to be the solution.

In the same way that it is hard to shift our view in order to *see* Great Bee, not just all those little moving bees, as one creature ~ in the same way it is hard to see the causes of what is called colony collapse. This collapse means that One Bee died. Usually one day the hive is simply empty. Being fastidiously clean, bees will not die in their hive, they fly away and we assume they therefore die. Sometimes their Queen is left since she would be too heavy to fly. Yes, they even leave their Queen. They leave it all, as if leaving a feast on the table half eaten. When you open the hive perhaps a few bees will be wandering around. No other bees or wasps will rob the honey of this hive. As we know, none of this is natural. Yet our habit of mind, these past hundred and fifty years or so, is to examine the parts, not to look at the whole. We are still doing that with this issue, we are looking for singular solutions, singular causes. We are looking at the little moving parts, not the whole. There are lots of moving parts, many toxins and interferences in our mostly unnatural landscapes and these make up an ecology that is much bigger than the sum of its parts.

This ecology for Bee would have to include the quality of air she flies through, the sound waves coursing through that air; many fragrances with chemical signatures of man-made origins that bear no resemblance to the scents of nature. The closer Bee is to urban dwellers a cacophony abounds, bird song is overwhelmed, the whole fabric of nature's aural and perfumed airways are pervaded with our noisy, smelly, mechanistic manners.

Bees bristle with sensors, enabling them to travel three miles from home base with ease, to gather a good crop. All that is in the air must affect them, all that sound, scent, radiation, fine metal particles that we spray into the air daily in some vain attempt to seed rain clouds ~ all the stuff our human-modern world has come to depend on, to take for granted. It is sobering to watch and to listen as so much that is natural, of nature, is overwhelmed by our 'sophisticated' ways.

Many of us grow up now far away from nature, far away from what is natural. We grow up in malls, in convenience stores, in movie theaters or in front of big home screens. We, like our landscape, have become industrialized. Our ears no longer register the incessant drone of traffic, fans, wheels running over all sorts of surfaces, rarely quiet. All our bells and whistles create havoc within nature's raw environments.

When we visit Nature, more than just the parts of us gets restored. When we visit wild places: ocean, mountain, valley, plain, moor or desert; when we stay a while, we know that something intangible within ourselves feels 'better'. We need raw nature to become whole again ourselves.

After World War I the returning soldiers were taught beekeeping. It was good work for them, quieting the body and mind, working alone outdoors with these loving wild ones. Bees know something about calming trauma; just to sit nearby and listen to the hum of hive soothes so deeply. To work with them calms even more. Working out on the heath, in the meadows and orchards these shell-shocked men could find dignity and grace within again. Just being out-of-doors, allowed to stay feral, let these men heal. More noise, working industrially, was not going to help at all. Trauma is sensitive to noise and bright lights. Too much noise and flashing bright lights can induce trauma. Bee hives, like children, need natural light and non-threatening sounds around them. So do we.

Just to listen, to gaze at dawn, to quietly absorb all around at twilight, touches us in a way that no urban or city-scape can do. Softly penetrating through all our senses we could say that sunset, moonrise, starshine touches our Soul. Of all the despairing people who have jumped off the Golden Gate Bridge, fragmented by sound and light, by not being heard or seen ~ not one of them jumped out toward Ocean. They all faced what had betrayed them, the urban landscape, the merely human world. I can understand that somewhere. Mother Nature does not betray us. It doesn't work like that.

What is brought forth to life here on this planet is inevitably in simpatico with the environment it is born into. If you pile leaves up against the curb and let them stay there, worms will appear in the leaf pile, not tadpoles, worms. The migrating monarch butterflies are born, as caterpillars, on or near milkweed plants which are all they can eat. They cannot come into being in a field of corn. This mutually beneficial, co-arising relationship underlies all life forms. When Air changes, when the mix of gases changes over aeons, when Soil changes, so do the type of animal and plant life that can live with that. Some migrate over space and time. Weather patterns and landscapes change, deserts grow, glaciers retreat, species migrate accordingly. Otherwise they mutate.

Our recent forays into genetic manipulation of plant and animal species appear to be pushing this curve. We have cultivated plants for centuries but never before have we been so disrespectful as to force a pairing between plant and animal, as we are now allowing in our labs and from there to our fields. This crosses an ethical barrier that causes us to move away from a sense of refinement in our lives and toward a greater sense of power and greed. Over the past hundred and sixty years or so we have shifted the whole slowly cultivated dynamic between ourselves and all of the rest of our world toward mutation, by our crass pursuit of bigger, better, bust. Toxins most readily harm soft organs, especially reproductive ones. They can change the exquisite chemistry of our glands. People exposed to chemical farming without proper protection have been known to become sterile or to have children that are not fully formed in utero. Cancers have increased throughout human bodies as our environment becomes comparably degraded.

Honey Bees have become susceptible to harm through intestinal troubles and mites, indicators of systemic weakening in the hive. Over the winter of 2006 into 2007 the American bee industry saw devastating losses of bees. Some big rig keepers lost 90% of their bees that winter. This has continued annually since and has now stabilized at 30-50% of hives being lost every year to CCD, colony collapse disorder. Pollination is a multi-billion dollar industry, not primarily about honey, but about fertilization of fruit crops. Industrially-farmed fruit needs bees to arrive when flowering and to go away afterward so sprays can be used that would kill them if they stayed. It's not just that either: it's about renting out your bees. Why leave them in one place when you can pack them up, stack them up, wrap them up and drive them either north/south or east/west and plop them in some monocultured field somewhere, cashing in on your 'pollinator units'. This is how industrial beekeepers make a living. They pimp One Bee. The hive weakens.

Death by a thousand cuts, I call it, this so-called colony collapse. We must be driving them demented. Just as our cows went crazy when their diet was altered to include meat (insultingly, the left over parts of themselves after slaughter). Cow doesn't eat meat. No wonder they got that mad cow disease. On their way to the highly refined foods of pollen and nectar, our Bees are overwhelmed with toxins and disoriented by our high beam, high intensity, bips and bleeps. Manipulation and industrialization go hand in hand. Even in the research world one solution to this colony collapse, lauded by many, is the genetic manipulation, the laboratory creation of a new strain of bee that is resistant to mites…sounds like some corn I heard about recently that is also resistant to all sorts of bugs, even to poisons that kill other plants. This is a counter-intuitive solution though. If the plants in your garden are weak you don't crossbreed them, you feed the soil they are in, strengthening the roots. Bugs don't go for strong plants, strong soil will take care of all that. Biodiversity will take care of that. Honey Bees need a great variety of nectar and pollen in the hive, not just oranges or almonds or even lavender but we plant miles of them without a thought to diversity, only to greater harvests, greater profit and control of a greater market.

'Bigger, better, bust' has been the trajectory of the industrial bee-keeping business. It may be the overriding trajectory of our culture and we are living in the years of 'bust'. The 'boom' is still reverberating in our ears, and our eyes lost sight of the forest while we were harvesting the trees. The mechanistic mind has to work in parts, little moving parts, it does not naturally see the whole. The industrial mind looks at the end product, seeking reliable, rapid, repeating profit; not sustainability, but continuous growth: keep it coming off the conveyor belt, more and faster every year. Everyone of us is completely used to finding honey at any corner store, grocery store or supermarket in the world. How can there be so much honey every day of the year? Where does it come from?

I have often wondered who decided that we have to live 'better', earn more, have more, each year after year, rather than finding out what we really need and staying steady with that instead. This stress seems redundant, or self-inflicted as a social norm and it may be having some chronic effects on us. It certainly seems to be changing our global climate system, our soil, our air and water.

It is as if we have always been running away, always reacting against our past, feeding our fears. In America the dust bowl days appall and fascinate, in Europe, the great wars. Landscapes are radically different now with our cities shining brighter than the stars. We no longer reference rivers and mountains but highways, airports and screens.

With the loss of this relationship comes a loss of caring. We tend to care for what comforts us. When what comforts us becomes a gizmo rather than a landscape, then, looking at that landscape, our mind mines it for parts to make our gizmo with. We stop caring about the landscape, we no longer see it whole. We are sniffing for the parts.

Along with this general degradation of our home base, planet Earth, comes a pervasive and smothering degradation of all other life forms as 'civilized' humans dominate the landscape. We no longer see our place within the larger fabric of Nature. We have paved over much of it and scalped much more. The farmlands are no longer naturally viable, no longer supporting a thick web of life forms, having been adulterated for so long with bigger, better chemicals that have caused our soil to go bust. It is the same strange story with so many of our resources in this country and across the globe. We are waking up rapidly to all this now but where were we before the world wide web? How could we simply not know?

I did not 'know' because I was too busy enjoying the *Feast*, tasting all that society offered that was cool, new, edgy, with no thought of others, entirely in my own bubble. It never occurred to me to worry about *source* ~ where coal came from, where petrol came from, where exhaust went ~ these were simply the methods of heat and transport we were all grateful for. With your own wheels you are free! This of course was one of the great mythic calls of America, her highways and cheap gas. You could go so far with so little! You could definitely get the hell out of here! You could up and go without hesitation there was so much room to roam, places to go, different foods to eat, music to hear.

When I grew up it was truly a patriotic act amongst my elders to enjoy the Feast! This was after rationing in Britain and the end to that was cause for great feasting. Trouble was, we forgot to leave the table, we became addicted ~ to sugar, to corn, to new grains made from prairie grasses, all new foods arriving in all new big bright shops, runny honey in bear-shaped plastic jars, 'fun for your kids and good for you' too! We all know this. I grew up when it was all new. I remember my mother coming home with frozen peas for the first time.

49

Amazing ~ and we had a fridge! The man with fresh vegetables stopped coming around with his cart. I missed feeding his horse. Eventually, even the milk man stopped delivering. Food got wrapped up. "At your convenience ma'am."

Food gets delivered in delicious nutritious tiny morsels within the honey bee hive. It comes without packaging. There is no waste. Outside the hive, bees live in light and air, gathering the finest of Nature's offerings: nectar, pollen and water. That is all they need to feed the eternal hive. Diversity is the key here: many kinds of nectar, many kinds of pollen meeting a vast array of magical juices within the gut of each little metaphysical honey bee. There is no competition in the hive of course, since it is a single creature, and naturally bees will settle about a mile or so apart from each other, half a mile at least.

Rows of hives are industrialized bees, perceived as 'livestock' and some counties give agricultural land tax status if you have them. Closer to town folks are wary and unsure of their relationship to bees, still mixing them up, as I did, with the decidedly unfriendly wasp. Everyone who sees a bee hive thinks about eating honey. Not everyone eating honey thinks about a bee hive. We are still sniffing for the parts, wildly seeking only that which pleases us. We have stopped hearing, stopped referencing, stopped even noticing the Holy. Inundated by noise and light, how can we find our way?

I try to keep my hive away from street lights at night so that starlight can touch it. Industrial noises disturb the comb through vibration. It is so sensitive, being the communication grid within, as well as a mass of cells. Each cell's rim is slightly thicker than the cell wall as the wax gets built up there. Bees walk along the rims of the cells, never getting their feet sticky with honey since that would trap them and eventually cause their untimely death. They walk along the rim of each cell tending its contents, baby bee or food storage. They are always in touch with each other through the wax web of communication. Whatever causes strong vibration: waggle dancing, incoming drones, a non-family member dropping by, is picked up by every bee through the 'wax wire web', the internal telegraph system that is a part of, yet pervades, the system of the hive. Queen's scent likewise pervades the comb, including the wax on each little bee's tiny bod. She rules through being everywhere at all times, serving and controlling, *solve* and *coagula*. Always this magic in the hive.

Precious things handled without respect quickly slip out of the non -ordinary into the ordinary, but truly they don't belong there. Precious things in the ordinary world lose their luster.

Great Bee in a box loses something of her shine, her innate life force dims. Wild ones do not do well in boxes and cages.

The bee box was invented in 1851 by a man called Langstroth. Queen rearing has become an industry in itself since then, a necessity for weak hives or impatient beeks. As in most cases, quantity over-whelms quality. The more honey we take, pollen we scrape, hives we rent, the weaker the health of our bees.

It is time to listen again to this messenger from God, for our own health is diminishing, no matter how much we have on our plates.

It takes a lot of spaciousness to lift up and see another view. For me it took stepping out of my stage hand life and into the robes of a Zen monk. I had been living at Zen Center in San Francisco, walking down the hill to the Opera House to work on the props crew by day and sometimes by night. Morning and evening I went to meditation, nights off work I went to study classes. I thought I would keep swinging between the two but I had not yet heard the garden call, that place where worlds meet. Opera season ended, I went to Tassajara.

Into the spaciousness and quiet comes an inner listening, which gradually ex-pands to encompass a radiant circle around me. I can hear for a hundred yards or so, a blue jay, a monk, which one! I move and the rustle of robes laps over everyone. We are each in the space of many others' circles of sensation. Monk, blue jay, gong. We overlap in this way.

Please take a moment to gaze into this image: it is called the Flower of Life.

It is made entirely of overlapping circles.

You may see a hexagon, triangles, petals, stars, yet it is all made of equal circles overlapping.

51

Drawing by Aliya Goldstein

Flower of Life

The symbolic meaning of this image is said to be that it represents perfect health. It is found in many spiritual centers, as mosaic or carved in stone, centuries old. There are many teachings here.

For one who prefers a simple approach, I contemplate this overlapping, this sphere of influence and connectivity. In the Buddhist teachings it is called Interdependence; in Hindu verses, the Web of Life. Both these teachings show us that we are not truly able to separate our actions from other overlapping spheres of influence that share this revolving planet. This image helps us to connect the dots, to shift our perception and to wonder: what other path can we choose that allows us to step back a little and take our place *amongst* others, rather than in place of them; amongst the wild ones and tall standing ones, rather than in place of them; *with* Nature, not in spite of it or by denying our future selves the renewing, the Soul healing, surely the right, to simply be in Nature, in natural sound, in natural air, drinking safe water from a stream.

If nothing else Wind will make sure we share what we put into Air. If nothing else Wave will come and dump our garbage back upon our doorsteps. If nothing else Earth will rock and cause us all to tremble. If nothing else Fire will come consuming in the wake of the consumers.

It isn't easy to see the whole, to notice how much your personal actions pervade others' lives. Many of us have little self control or clear intention, yet we do have an influence, as everything has on us. The edges of our spheres are porous, information passes through and our senses inform us of all around, like wax comb.

The Flower of Life indicates that our perfect health, the perfection of health on this particular planet, has a lot to do with the balanced overlapping of spheres of influence. No one dominates the whole, together a whole comes into being: a flower amongst flowers.

The connective tissue of this discussion is flowering; how we flower, how bee hives flourish. One of the great revelations of the Genome project was that the same gene which causes a flower bud to open, also causes the soft organs of a human fetus to open. Your kidneys and other organs literally flower into life within the womb. Gazing into this image of perfect health, this Flower of Life, we see equal spheres interconnecting to create a whole that is greater than its parts and whose resonance is Holy.

Bees know all about flowers and flowers open for them. They have symbiotic spheres of influence. Symbiosis is true sophistication. No harm is done, all is mutually beneficial.

The key to this flowering is listening, coiling, waiting, for the moment when all is in alignment, friendly, co-arising.

It is this mutual beneficence that seems to be missing in our lives. As a species we have stepped out of our niche, out of symbiosis. Most of all we have stepped out of respect and this shows up in our language every day.

In my twenties there were just vegetables and fruit. In my thirties I noticed 'fresh fruit'. In my forties, after a few years away from the ordinary world, I discovered 'conventional' vegetables and fruit. Then I began to see the lie, the deception, the linguistic training we were being subject to. It is generally called marketing.

When I first emigrated to the States I wanted to drive from 'sea to shining sea', which I did on ribbons of tarmac slicing through vast open lands. It was beautiful, except for the billboards and they were ubiquitous. Right out in the proverbial 'middle of nowhere' as we were 'slip slidin' away', advert after advert vied with raw nature for our attention in very unsubtle ways. I trained myself not to look at them, never to engage in reading them. I had to actually learn to stay engaged with the real landscape, rather than checking them out as potentially 'natural' intrusions. Now I see these billboards were the precursor of personal screens. Today marketing companies crawl the web and send personalized ads to your private in-box. The language is pervasive and persuasive.

In my fifties the USDA brought out organic food labeling. The lie seemed complete. No ordinary food is organic. Conventional (meaning normal?) food does not need to be labeled. The same trajectory is in place for genetically engineered or modified food. Now we label to deny modernity, to defend the true meaning of 'natural'. Our language is pervaded with the trappings of this lie. When climates change, even linguistic ones, mutation can arise. When the climate in our belly changes will mutations arise? If so how shall we name that?

This naming is very powerful. We can call it progress, we can call it wrong. Whatever we call it can't name it, unless we lift up and change our perspective to get a more encompassing view. We know we can't solve a problem where it lies, we have to look down on it, see it from above, taking in the whole darn thing.

Then we can see that it is not that we wish to stop progress, or that we wish to blame, but that we wish to speak the language of respect.

CHAPTER FIVE

The Language of Respect

When the Roots are bound, the Tree cannot bear fruit.

*O*ne of the reasons I went into the monastery was to tame my speech. I was a very angry young woman caged in an urban environment I could never master. I drank, I swore, I was a reckless teenager, and it took years to knock some sense into this head! I was kind and gentle too...I had my moments. I just had to reverse which ones came up most. The Buddhist teachings train you through body, speech and mind. At Tassajara, body was tamed by schedule: you turned up, sat down, sat up straight and stayed like that...session after session, day after day. Speech was clearly an issue with all incoming monks. We were instructed to remain silent!

What I did not know then, but abide by now, is that I was seeking this language of respect. This language, available in all tongues, is about relationship. For those of us who grow up speaking English it mostly means adjusting our use of the word 'the'. In our sentences this is called an article. By using it we make an article of what we are naming, placing it over there to be looked at and examined, counted and named, but not held close so it can be experienced. When we drop this article and say Bee, rather than *the* bee. Better still, Great Bee. Moon, rather than *the* moon. Tree rather than *the* tree: then we begin to experience Bee, Moon and Tree as we would do Jane, Susan or Jim. This languaging of our relationship to other spheres of influence in our lives, that connect and overlap us all, this way of speaking more intimately, changes things a lot.

At first it feels weird and artificial, like something kind of woo-woo or just plain strange. If we think a moment about that, we might feel sad to recognize how far away we are from the throb of Nature. So we might try it out and see what happens. What *does* happen is just as strange. Nature comes closer. It is a bit different at first, this sense of real communication with Moon, Wind, Tree. Removing the article is like lowering your arm, no longer keeping your distance.

Life gets personal.

This language of respect causes us to name our hives Eden, Freya, Gaia, as we name our children. We have chosen, no ~ we have been chosen ~ to care for them, to tend them and to help them thrive in an outer environment we feel we have no control over. We live in stress-filled times and adrenals are flooded, inside and outside the hive. Our senses are overloaded and we think we should do more. Everything about this lie is bigger, better, bust.

There really is no need for any of us to use more resources, eat more food, have bigger homes or more toys than last year. The Art of Life has to do with symbiosis. Enough is just that, plenty. Bees know this, all species but humans know this. We have crossed a Rubicon of time and now we are asked to base our present actions not upon our past, not upon our fears, but upon our future realistic vision, co-arising from our overlapping spheres.

Symbiosis has a particular geometry, it is circular, spiral in nature. Industry has a particular geometry too; it is square, stackable in its design. If we are going to shift from the industrial model to a symbiotic one this might be an interesting thing to consider. Commercial bee hives are square and stackable, convenient for loading and hauling, for adding on high rise honey boxes. Cities also cluster together work forces in boxes stacked in high risers.

The geometry fits the paradigm.

My head reels here since it tends to get caught up in the idea that, because I don't do math, therefore I can't understand geometry. Once I get over that, a whole world of wonder opens up. I still can't do more than rudimentary math, but I have a great relationship to numbers and to shape. These numbers and shapes turn up in all of Nature: all roses are based on the number five, like apples, for example. Daffodils are related to number six. You just have to look closely and you can see that, no real hard math required! This is another language in itself, the language of rhythms within Nature; the language of deep relationship between our Earth, Moon and the other planets that cycle around our Sun with us. Sacred Geometry is all about describing those relationships, the way Leonardo Da Vinci does with his Vitruvian Man in a circle. It's about ratio and form. Mostly, it's about observation and curiosity! For me it's all about great correspondences.

A square corresponds to the number four. It has straight firm boundaries, all the same length. This is a good shape to contain other straight-edged things in, or to stack, but not to grow in. Five corresponds to our senses and the five elements, five oceans and so forth, often considered the number of Earth. The same drawing of the man in the circle describes this well. Five is about the great Feast, all we can experience through those five senses. Six is about the heart. Any quick study of various systems of correspondences: numerology; astronomy and astrology; elements and organs; shapes and colors and all that, will give you a sense of the incredible, intrinsic beauty of this world we live in and how it all fits together. In a pure way ~ far from soppy romantic views, projections or wishings ~ Sacred Geometry is an elegant language of describing Beauty.

Inside the hive the geometry is hexagonal and the paradigm one of inclusiveness and harmony. Wild bees don't nest closer than half a mile apart. They give each other space. Their spheres of influence and harvest overlap, yet are exclusive. Birds of prey likewise overlap their hunting grounds but nest within their own bounds.

What happens in the collective mind when we nest too close and become over-crowded? Doesn't this cause more stress? Is this a factor in the timing of a swarm? Is swarming a stress release as well as a reproductive act? If we keep adding on boxes and preventing a swarm are we increasing stress? Is there a 'natural' limit to the size of a city, a hive, a corporation? If so it would probably fit best with the geometry of symbiosis, the geometry of respect.

This is what it means, to me, to think outside the box.

Scattered throughout my challenging childhood are moments of pure magic, most of them out-of-doors. My father was one of the late great English gentlemen, a naturalist, a scholar and craftsman. He opened up the outside world to me of which I was mortally afraid when very small. My early years were restricted to house and garden, with him we went rambling and encountered so much more. Gradually I learned to take in the context of environment and its animals: to hear a sound and know to listen for a response across the meadow; to see a fawn and know to wait 'til its mother had also gone by, not to separate them or cause alarm.

Reality TV in my youth was hosted by David Attenborough, Jaques Cousteau, and Carl Sagan. I drank it up. Here was the whole world, and the reason for TV! I hid behind the couch when *Dr Who* was on, but sat right up in front for a Nature show.

In later years I spent months reading and re-reading the pages of Fritjof Capra's *The Tao of Physics*, which stretched my mind as no other book had done. Having just left college I was free to read and study what I wished. More and more I was drawn toward understanding the patterns, the interweaving of life cycles and our place in this world. More and more I fell in love with this planet, this Earth and all her awesome ways. Traveling showed me her beauty.

I kept reading and studying. Theatre life is so conducive to this. It's true that when a show is in production it is all consuming but when it gets going, all being well, a good run gives the company a very steady rhythm, a steady paycheck and lots of time alone. Work usually starts around 5pm. It's a good life!

I was fortunate to seek work in the U.S. first when the 1970's gas rationing was going on. All systems seek internal balance and what may look like hardship to some will always be of good to others. It's all relative after all. A show in Miami had to close, no one was driving! A quick tour through Canada (no rationing!) was planned and because the sound person did not want to do a 'Bus and Truck' ~ usually referred to as 'Truss and Buck' ~ eventually I got the gig. There is no time for reading on a Bus and Truck, not for the crew when we are flown ahead in tiny bi-planes so all will be ready for the cast's arrival. They get to sleep on a bus. Tough choices here! No, no time at all when you are doing two cities a week. The pay off came later on the national tour when we spent months in one place. Chicago was the best. So many book stores! Three, or was it four, months of steady steady study study.

All this study had to be balanced out with contemplation and meditation. Study alone cannot fly, it needs a visceral medium, it needs to become a felt sense, an experience, a skill perhaps or a knowing. This 'knowing' seems to come directly from Nature into us through the unspoken language of respect which I simply call 'meeting'. We can study all we want about a particular animal but until we meet it, really meet it, we won't know anything at all. Jane Goodall taught us that. Here again we find the twins of looking at parts or seeing a whole.

To truly meet another living being we have to see it whole, in all its overlapping contexts, the flower within a flower.

I find this hard to do. I notice my mind wanting to create hard boundaries where there may not be any. I catch it taking an image or 'fact' and pushing it into a framework of thought I am playing with, like a child pushing in the wrong piece of a jig-saw puzzle, determined to make it fit. Constantly I have to step back and get out of the way, to allow what I am meeting to present as it wishes, from its own side. No pushing, no pulling. This is where meditation comes in so handy. After a few years you get the hang of just letting things fall where and as they will, without having to control it all, without jumping ahead to make sure it all fits into your personal mindbox. You get tolerant of things being 'out of shape'. You get past your fears.

Sitting for hours close to my hive watching and listening, gazing and contemplating, I began to take in the vast activity within that I could not see but knew about. Lifting bars of comb, peering into individual cells to see the content (green pollen! purple! baby bee! honey!), I am fascinated by the parts and the movement, the slow dance-like flow of activity that is live honeycomb. Only when I sit with her can I reach with mind's eye to the foragers down the hill on rosemary and on apple trees. Green pollen from eucalyptus trees? Red bud offers her own. Great Bee casts her sphere of influence wide, overlapping Bee from other hives, sharing in the bounty. She is seething slowly within the hive and working the hillsides too. As I slow my mind and let it rest in the center of my chest I am able to become aware of all this. I am able to meet Great Bee. She has an awesome splendor.

There have been very few times I have really met another creature, even possibly a human, at this level of wholeness. I am not sure I have completely met her yet. I wonder if I am able to comprehend, to meet with all my senses, the depth of beauty displayed within a hive. I think I can only approach, so I do.

I have felt this awe in the face of Nature before. In India I finally overcame my lifelong fear of spiders by being struck by the beauty of a massive red and yellow hunter in her tree-adorning web. First I saw Beauty ~ then I saw Spider. A pause, and Beauty won. Nature meets us in this way, taking us by surprise, lighting up evergreens at night with Stars, making Spring look like Christmas; spinning us around at sunset to see orange Moon rising over ancient Alps. She surely takes our breath away; old breath, stale breath, leaving us full of fresh Air. Life is curved, moves in swirls, Wind and Water borne. We are children of Earth's Weather.

When Weather was different here, human form did not arise. We are children of Earth's weather, blessed by many heavens. We exist on this planet within the context of this solar system within the context of our Milky Way. Life is curved, moves in swirls, Wind and Water born ~ flowers overlapping flowers creating Flowers.

Communication does not come easily to us since we are not used to sharing through the language of respect. It is so hard to train the eye to take in, rather than to calculate or judge and weigh, what it sees; to see the landscape, not the billboards. It is as if we are forever hungry, never satisfied, always seeking more. This distortion of our view, toward sniffing for resources rather than relating to living breathing landscapes, changes us, our words, our vocabulary and our underlying intent. Our intention is rarely kind in the eye of Nature, we are still so absorbed by the Feast. Everything about our global financial markets is based upon our sniffing, our snatching and grabbing of all that belongs here. To satisfy this feasting over the past very few hundred years we humans have killed one third of all life on this planet.

Making every effort to step away from this Feast in my own life I have to find a new way to consider a few things. How can I live more simply? What do our bees need? Both of those questions led to issues of housing. For me it was time to move and for my bees it was time to build a new hive; one *they* would want me to build. Yet how can a human, who corresponds with the number five, communicate with a creature that corresponds to the number six? Through the sixth sense, of course, how else?! No other way would I meet Great Bee. I needed her guidance, it was to be her home.

This sixth sense is a culmination of all the others, the regular five. In the same way the training of a monk accentuates five areas of deep practice that culminate in a sixth, Wisdom. This same 'wisdom channel' opens up in us whenever we sit quietly, not closing our senses to the outside (or inside) world, but letting all come to rest and simply noticing what happens. It's about gazing, not looking; about sound waves moving, not hearing. This receptiveness, this inter-dependence is experiential, is felt, when we sit in meditation or contemplation for a long time.

The five 'senses' we studied and practiced in the monastery were: generosity, ethical conduct, patience, diligence and meditation. These engender and lead to wisdom. In our ordinary five senses we hear, see, touch, smell and taste and these together create a sixth sense that gives rise to a language between life forms.

I get a sense of things, I get curious and ask questions and then sit and wait and wonder, 'til some kind of response reveals itself. This can be through thought form, vision, hearing or simply a sense of meeting a view not reached before. I am quite familiar, even comfortable, with mystery and wonder.

I think it useful to open up pathways between us as humans and other creatures, vegetable, animal or mineral, that share our world, through a language of respect. We will always be subject to the tendency toward projection, yet if we still our minds enough, don't go fishing for a certain outcome and are prepared to be made uncomfortable, then maybe we will be able to meet whatever effort is being made toward us from the rest of life on Earth. Certainly Great Bee did not come to make me comfortable.

She arrived incognito, subtle and charming. This alone should have given me clear warning! One bee, one little regular lovely bee came visiting during morning meditation. It was early winter, 2006. I was in retreat integrating and recovering from five years of training in trauma. We all responded in our own ways to the events of 9/11/01. I went to back to school. Study and practice!

In one of the courses I attended, we learned to access perceptual states, various points of view, by aligning with and becoming friendly with certain animals as archetypes. Into my morning stillness came a quiet buzzing, a small Honey Bee who showed herself within my crown chakra. The regular meeting with each chakra had become part of my morning practice, a sort of internal cleansing and checking in that I find useful and refreshing. Usually I start low and work up through each flowering chakra, getting a sense of how things are, meeting any disturbance or joy as I go. This day I was surprised by Bee, delighted really, wow! I just got visited by Bee today! Hmmm.

I forgot about that, upon standing up probably, and had no further thought 'til the next morning when ~ there she was again. I was taken by surprise, again. Hmmm. Wait and see, it might be my own wild mind playing. Next day I wondered of course if Bee would turn up. As I began my practice, long before I got up to the crown, a very strange sensation came over me, over my whole torso. It felt as if hundreds and hundreds of bees were slowly crawling up my body, waves of them coming and landing and walking up toward my head. It was very weird, I was not sure if I was just 'having a moment' where maybe my body was too hot or something; it was just plain strange. After a while, maybe ten minutes or so, hundreds of bees assembled in the flower of my crown chakra and piled up there like the knobs on Buddha's head, like a skep hive. I thought I had really lost it again. Hmmm.

Rather than lose it over losing it, I thought to speak to Bee. Every day for two weeks, there they were and no response at all, just humming along. Then at the beginning of the third week Queen showed up. I knew nothing about bees and had no notion that it takes sixteen days for a colony to hatch a queen.

Something was going on here that seemed authentic. I was not making this one up.

Queen talked. Her Majesty had a lot to say, and at first it was mostly about trauma. She talked about fragmentation of the soul, a wearing out of life force and a sense of forcing in the adrenals. I only later understood that our Bees were in trauma too. This was the winter of the devastating colony collapse. I have heard that a lot of folks got visited by Great Bee that winter and many others since. Most of what I heard through this sixth sense way of listening within, conversing with an archetype, meditating on the essence of Honey Bee (such words skirt an experience not easily caught and they cannot describe it), most of it had to do with glandular stress.

The cry, the remedy most requested, was for *Starlight*.

Though the chemical issues of recent decades are of cumulative and, consequentially dangerous, proportions ~ despite all this the underlying stress was light, lack of natural light, especially starlight. The 'message' I was getting was that we all, bees ~ people, trees and critters ~ *all* suffer from a chronic lack of natural light, of natural rhythm, and are stressed by all the street lights, stadium lights and airports that obliterate our stars at night over so much of our land. This seemed really important to 'my' bees.

Stars and sacred geometry go together. My dad taught me that long ago, and he knew everything as far as I could tell. He understood the seasons and stars and snowflakes and where to get comb honey when we needed it. Aligning with the stars, making sure you are taking all into account, is what the word 'consideration' means: con/with : sider/sidereal (of the stars). We use it all the time and still leave all the lights on! We are so in-con-*sider*-ate, so out-of-sync with our stars, with the rhythms of life, *Rhythms of Vision*, as Lyall Watson called them.

We can tilt, we are already tilting together toward a new respect, a renewed respect with our home and our Honey Bee. It is the issue of home, of housing we most need to address. If we are going to stop stacking and packing we must design a new way based on the honey-comb hexagon, not upon axis base and high-rises. My personal feeling is that this six-ness is the new geometry, the new paradigm and that the prevailing packaging of goods within the structure of four, solely to serve the feast of the five senses, has to give way. Our addictive habits, our stubborn insistence on continuing, even developing, toxic energy sources in order to keep us all fired up have to be tamed. We have over-eaten, given in to greed for too long and now it is time to leave the Feast. We can master our senses, train them and refine them, not give in to their bottom line. I think if we don't do this we will simply not survive. Nature will not be able to afford us. As we know it is hard to see this whilst still feasting. If we are to get out of the industrial box (four), rather than continue to indulge in the nuances of feasting (five), we must shift into a new view; a view connected to the heart (six).

To get from four to six you go three dimensional, to the cube. Take a flat square, lift it into a cube and then look down upon it to see the six pointed flower. No need to stay linear and work through five. We can leave the Feast at last! Lift up! Out of the box and into the Flower of Life.

In the monastery we chanted: Great Wisdom beyond Wisdom, Heart Sutra.
On one level it's about going beyond your five senses…'no nose no tongue no taste no smell'…and about not getting caught, hooked in, deluded by the Feast. We are so

easily distracted through our senses from what we actually wish to do, especially in matters pertaining to our long term aspirations and commitments. We can wake up ten years later and wonder, "Where was I before this sequence began? What was I going to do before I lost track?" On the meditation mat daily, mind wanders, bell rings and again a realization of following distraction arises! It is hard to go beyond.

Only by seeing through it, seeing the lie that you need the Feast (that is the lie), can you be free enough to choose not to engage. Quality will always triumph over quantity when you make that choice.

It sounds hard and can be, if you want it to be, but my experience is that it simply brings me home to my center. I become present, I am here. This is the feeling of number six. If you stretch out your arms like clock hands at ten to one, then your arms are 90° apart. You can feel the restrictive quality of that in your body. Then open your arms so that the clock reads ten to two and you can feel the inclusion of the wider angle which is 120°. This is the visceral sense of the shift between four and six.

Four has angles of 90°, Six has angles of 120°. Four says, "Mine!" Six says, "Ours."

Great Bee never says, "Mine!" She is a collective noun with compound eyes and a life force that need never be extinguished.

She lives within the geometry of six

Drawing by Jonas Goldstein

66

and somehow I sense this connects her to our stars that she so clearly needs for wholeness.

My question became: Which rhythms in the hive show me how she relates to which stars? Where were celestial influences showing up in the hive? I simply couldn't find it in the shape of honeycomb, in the space of the hive.

It had to be in the timing.

CHAPTER SIX

Considerations

"As above, so below." Hermes Trismegistus

The gestation cycles for the three different bees in a honey bee hive are all different. They must be linked to different cyclic influences, I thought.

The gestation period of a Queen bee is 16 days.

The gestation period of a Worker bee is 21 days.

The gestation period of a Drone bee is 23-25 days.

The easiest one to pin down here is the Worker's cycle of 21 days which we know to be the spin cycle of our Sun. It takes 21 Earth days to revolve on its own axis, so 21 of our days is one Sun day. This is why that great movie about the plight of our bees was called *Queen of the Sun*. It's the Workers who are Sun-oriented most, they are born to Sun's cycle.

The Queen cycle of 16 days is not so easy to pinpoint in our stars above, and it took a long time for me to let its rhythm reveal itself. I knew that her full and natural life cycle of 8 years was linked to the orbital dance that Venus and Earth make together in the skies. It is said in some ancient traditions that Honey Bee is a gift from Venus, our sister planet. Those Melissae of ancient Greece said so. Often in my readings I find reference to this extraordinary relationship between Venus and Earth. Venus corresponds to the number six, as does the Heart. Earth corresponds to number five, the sensory Feast. This again echoes the movement from the Feast toward the Heart. This is our transition now.

Venus and Earth are what we call sister planets because our orbits are linked together, though we spin in opposite directions. Venus is closer to Sun than we are, so she runs around him faster than we do. Every now and then we three create a line through space, we are conjunct. This happens every time Venus passes us by, at one exact point we meet. If you trace the points at which we meet out there in the sky, you will find yourself tracing a five pointed star. This movement of Venus and Earth together around our Sun gives us the pentangle symbol; isn't that great?!

This is what sacred geometry is ~ the description of Beauty, of Nature, in action! It takes eight years for these planets to draw a pentangle in the sky, the life span of a healthy Queen Bee.

The Drone cycle got my attention right away because it was not exact. Since when is anything in a hive not exact? What was that about? It turns out that the same planet, Venus, takes her pretty time traveling through the skies, dancing with some constellations longer than others. Venus takes between 23 and 25 days to pass through a constellation, such as Taurus or Libra. I was really amazed when I found that out. It makes me wonder if research would show this exact relationship within the hive: if Drone eggs laid during a longer Venus cycle take longer to hatch accordingly. How does that make a difference within the Drones' internal juices?

We know that the different constellations affect the hive according to the element they correspond with. When our Moon is in an Earth sign, such as Taurus, root activity is encouraged in the plant world and in the hive, comb building. Fire signs encourage fruiting in the plants and gathering of nectar in the hive. Water sign days indicate leaf growth and the making of honey. Air sign days promote flowering and the gathering of pollen.

The health of the hive has a lot to do with the diversity of sperm from the Drones during nuptial flights. Is it possible that the health of the Drone is linked to the strength of celestial influence in the hive? In other words, are our bees stronger if their hive is able to receive Starlight? Since their very life cycles are linked to stars it would seem quite probable that their request for Starlight is authentic. We may need it too.

So far we have the cycles of Sun and Venus in the hive, but we have not found an aha! for the 16 days of our Queen's gestation. To find this I went back to observation within the hive. I wanted to know how Queen moved. Was there a pattern to her movement? If so, I would see it in her egg laying. I could see it in the brood comb she had already laid ~ our Queen ever moves in spirals. Another swirl of life reveals its beauty.

Spirals are the geometry of our biology and our universe. We see it in fern, nautilus, sunflower and Milky Way; it is in the way trees fans out leaves so all share raindrops and sunshine. Spiral is so simple and elegant, described as the Fibonacci scale, even the math is approachable! It goes like this:

$$0 : 1 : 1 : 2 : 3 : 5 : 8 : 13 : 21 : 34 : 55 : 89 : 144...$$

Each number is the sum of the previous two numbers, you simply keep adding them to each other. Brilliantly simple, naturally.

Moon snail

Fibonacci fern

73

I still didn't get it. Where was the number 16 in here? Not.

I could not believe that there was no connective tissue between the life cycle of a Queen Bee and some aspect of sacred geometry. Wanting to find it in the spiral I had to step back from forcing an idea onto, rather than learning from Nature. I wanted to build a simple, thoughtful home for this engaging creature and to find the clues for it from honeycomb life, not from mine.

I tried out a couple of other top-bar hives, at least we all agreed on this basic design as being a worthy offering. The details could vary widely. Sam's, the one he started me off with, was shall we say, rustic. Chris traded time for a Spikenard Farm hive which I found too fussy, having mite trays and observation portals and all sorts of fancy stuff. I wanted something right in the middle: simple, elegant and kind.

Then he showed me a very fancy and heavy hive he called the 'golden mean hive'. What was that? I knew about the golden rule for sure (do no harm), but the golden mean? It's a ratio, the ratio of Beauty. The numbers are 1:1.618. In other words, if laying out a temple, one side would be 1.618 times the length of the other side of the rectangle.

The proportion, the ratio of *One to One point Six* sings.

I dare to say that the gestation period of a Queen Bee is not just 16 days but is exactly 16.18 days.

She is born to the golden mean, she is an expression of the golden mean.

It turns out that this Golden Mean is also expressed within the geometry of the pentangle. If you draw a pentangle within a pentangle, the smaller one inside will be inverted and in ratio to the larger one of 1:1.6. Then you can draw one inside that and it will be upright again and also in this ratio. You can keep drawing endlessly of course, and this sequencing describes fractals. It is all so astonishingly elegant!

Pondering all this I step back into meditation, clearing the mind so all can settle in and flower. This Great Bee is something else. In her form as Queen Bee she attains a biological perfection unrivaled in our world. She eats a food so pure there is no waste yet she lays her own weight in eggs every day in high summer. In her form as archetype she speaks of Starlight and the need to heal our glandular systems, including our Earth's glandular system which we call Weather. As an archetype she sits in the pineal gland, the 'seat of the Soul', and indicates the state of our Soul through her penetrating vision. Her girls indicate the social condition, the community and Drones as ever report on incoming influences. Much can be learned from Great Bee in this way, if we would but listen.

The greatest of all Buddhist teachings, the Prajña Paramita ~ compressed, haiku style, into our Heart Sutra ~ talks of that which is beyond duality; that which is beyond this world of right and wrong, listening and hearing, beyond the senses, far beyond the Feast.

There we find not nothing, not emptiness, but All that is, and it is Female. The Mother of All, she is called, the perfect, pervading, encompassing Mother, the Perfection of Wisdom.

Queen Bee is quite simply the closest expression of that perfection I have met on this Earth.

Shockingly she is in trouble, asking for such a simple thing as a clear night sky, perhaps so we can see more clearly too. The perspective we get when lying down under a clear star-studded sky is both one of smallness and one of belonging.

How many of us see this aspect of our Mother nowadays? I have met the same sense of the Holy when with our Bees. They are dying. The Holy in our world is dying.

If it is true, on any level at all, that God speaks only to Honey Bees, it would seem that He is withdrawing His messenger.

It may be that we are no longer worthy to care for the Holy. If we don't leave the Feast and enter into the Heart very soon, we too may experience colony collapse. Perhaps we think we are not worthy somehow. Is it possible that we have already fragmented ourselves too much for our Souls to recover? I don't think so. I believe we can make great changes in our lives. Many of us have already done so.

I believe that our future health depends on the Holy being respected, revered and realized within all life. Our ways of living need not deny our Soul. We need not trash our land in order to survive, we need not poison our fields in order to feed the world. It is our rank disregard of the Holy that is poisoning our world. Don't worry ~ soon the medics, scientists and brain mappers will encounter our Queen, they will have to recognize the existence of Soul. I wonder what they will hear. Hmmmm.

This presence of the Holy and our diverse invitations to it can be seen and heard in all our sacred architecture: our mosques, temples, churches and granges. With lift of ceilings, slant of light, the way internal space is laid out all describe a sense of reverence. There is a life force within the space of great places of worship that exudes, pervades and uplifts us all. In the Zen tradition the architecture, being Japanese, has surprisingly straight lines all gently lifted and slightly curved to take the edge away. Within the zendo, tatami mats and rice paper windows provide a soft quiet light throughout the day. The lines are simple, the practice is called 'serene reflection' and the meditation hall reflects this, invites it, describes it.

The zendo at Tassajara was the inspiration for much of the design of the hive I ended up building for Her Majesty and we call it Temple hive. The internal space is offered open and corresponds with the spiral, the Fibonacci scale. The bars inset just below the roof line without any fuss or gaps between them. There is no mite tray, no observation portal, no pollen catcher, no queen excluder, none of that, just a clean empty space on a very nice birchwood dance floor. This floor extends out from the base of the hive like the engawa around the zendo where a monk could do walking meditation if sitting was painful; like a southern veranda. The proportions of this floor are 1:1.6. There is much to engage in at the wide entrance to this hive. A long low roof, also cut to the golden mean, overhangs the 'dance floor' protecting the entrance from rain and sun alike, adding a little shade or warmth, since it is a second cover. Long front lines are all beveled at 30° to soften the edge. The effect is a little Frank Lloyd Wright, grand master of form and emptiness.

It took three years and far more attempts to get this hive right. In the end the riddle was no riddle and it took so long because "I don't do math". I can only think about numbers and that's not the same. The whole process was such a learning curve! First I had to learn how to handle a chop-saw...not too bad, but very noisy. Then came a table-saw, a terrifying and unforgiving invention that I could not do without.

So many mistakes, so much wood offered to Fire. This numbers thing really does make my head spin.

Lying down in frustration one night, asking myself where was the Fibonacci scale in these standardized board feet of wood? I am building a six-based house with four-based materials. Lift up! Go three dimensional…it has to be in the end piece, the dimensions had to show up there. I had the top width of 21", to honor the girls and their relationship with Sun. Since it was a trough, the ends of course were shaped as a trapezoid with slanting sides. I chose to cut these sides at 30° since that angle represents a hexagon. The trough thus becomes half a hexagon.

I wondered, if I had this right, could it be that the bottom width was 8 and the slanting sides 13? I was so excited I jumped out of bed, got dressed, drove down to my workshop, opened up the shed and took out the tape measure. Alleluia!! Praise be! Praise Bee, yes indeed, we had it right there…the sequence of the Fibonacci scale, the part that goes 8:13:21, those were the dimensions of the sides of the trapezoid that shaped the trough. The internal space of the hive was simpatico with the spiral; it described one.

It takes a while sometimes, but somehow in the end at moments like that it's worth all the heartache and headache. When Beauty shines she is unmistakeable. She has to be invited in though and we must prepare the way.

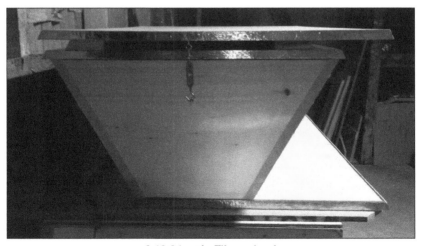

8:13:21 ~ the Fibonacci scale

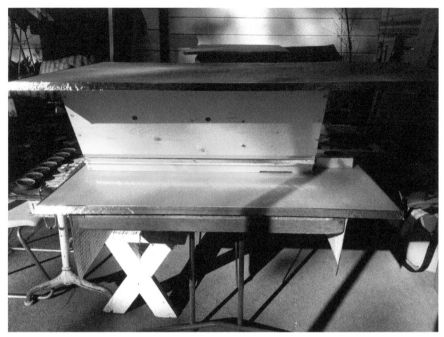

Temple Hive

It is my belief that all the poisons pervading our world are already beyond our control in their compound long-term effect. We have no idea what that will be on the land, in the oceans or within our own bodies. I also believe that we can stop engaging in this toxic Feast and use the old-fashioned boycott to turn our attention elsewhere. Yet ~ we are bound to make huge collective decisions very soon about our future and if we do not consider the Holy in our discussion we will be missing the mark.

I finally went down to get Freya. I knew it was a risk to move her hive so far, over eighty miles. The comb was thick and strong and I had not broken the seal of propolis anywhere by opening it up at all for months. She was as strong and secure as she could be. I wanted cloudy, even rainy days for the transition since all her bees would tend to be quieter then. I told the folks how to seal her up the night before and went to pick her up one Monday. I had lined up a soft ride ~ or so I thought! Confusions over vehicles so early in the mission gave me a heads up that this might not happen. I went down anyway to visit some children at Eden's hive where we talked about Bee and Beauty. After lunch I went over with another top-bar beek to pick her up.

Freya's hive was well wrapped so I lifted the lid to check, since there should be no bees above the bars ~ and there were a hundred girls or so, wondering what was going on. It was entirely my own fault. The last time I closed her up I either did not notice, or ignored, a tiny gap between two bars. Once closed up below those bees found the only possible escape and were wandering around on top of the bars under the inner cover. I couldn't move them. I wasn't going to sweep them off and leave them behind. The whole timing seemed off and the energy of the folks who had been hosting her was passively hostile. I could feel why she did not want to stay. I decided to open her up again, let her breathe and come down later when maybe, maybe, things would be calmer.

Two days later I drove down again with a strong man who knew nothing about bees. Clearly the host knew nothing either, despite his year of education with them. His repetitive request for honey revealed his inner paradigm: all this and what's in it for me? He was still angry when we arrived on the spring equinox, a rainy overcast day that was kind enough to let us move this hive without raindrops falling at the same time. Amazingly these two men got the hive into the van. Then came the shove. "NO BUMPS!" I cried as he firmly attempted to shut the door. I smelt honey. I was furious.

A journey of Kafka-esque qualities continued as I drove the angry, upset hive up Highway 1, around Devil's Slide and over the Golden Gate Bridge. After that I felt that whatever damage was done was done, and the worst must be over.

The van did not actually overheat to the point of blowing up or seizing the engine, but it did come very close, 'til Andrew found the fan unplugged and did the right thing. After that it was all pretty easy. By dusk the hive was on her new table under a persimmon tree to be left 'til dawn and then opened.

What I saw at dawn was pure carnage. Oozing honey dark with the bodies of thousands of dead bees coming out of the entrance, thick on the floor as far as my hive tool could reach. Freya was groaning. I was quiet in my mind for I felt her presence still strong though what I saw was horrible. What to do? What one thing could I do to help her now? I thought to lift each bar of comb out of this hive and place them in a new one, the ones that were not broken. I did not know how many broke yet, but moving them, breaking the seal of propolis, felt overly invasive. I wanted a simpler intervention.

Then I remembered that I don't screw the trough to the floor, precisely so I can lift it when needed. I fasten it all with turnbuckles instead. I hadn't needed to before, but I did now and was glad of that simplicity. I persuaded two men to lift the body of the hive away from the old floor which I simply slid out from under. Then I slid in three railings to set the hive on so it could drain any broken comb and I could see how much damage had been done.

On the floor was a whole comb, the last one down the far end of the hive. It had oozed down across the whole floor which was thick with honey and bees and grubs and so much loss. I knelt down to look at the rest of the comb in the hive. None of it was draining, it was all ok! Wow! I waited for half an hour to be sure and I know that hurt the brood by making it cold for so long, but then I persuaded the guys to come back again and, as they lifted Freya up one more time, I slipped under her a new birch dance floor.

For two weeks dead bees and larvae were dragged to the door and kicked out day and night while no pollen came in at all. What the foragers were bringing in was sap with which they made enough propolis to glue the hive to the new floor within a week. After three weeks pollen started coming in, guard bees took up positions at the front door, the hum descended to easier tones and against all odds Freya was alive and strong.

When I picked her up I had spent time with her quietly before we began, reminding her of that connection she has with the wild and awesome Mother of Perfection. It seemed only possible to me that she would agree to this journey if we treated her with respect, never forgetting the bridge Bees offer us to the Divine.

I know that the only reason that comb broke was because one person was angry, impatient and disrespectful. I sat with all the death and destruction at my feet for a long time before I started, as she did, to clean up and move forward.

I have heard that the Divine is ever-forgiving, I think that must be true.

Freya's blessings were gentle as she kissed me on cheek and brow, adjusting my view.

To be stung by Great Bee, to be called by her, is a strange path to Starlight. It is a path of Heart. It is a somewhat painful path to be honest. It is not easy to see so clearly how unkind our human world actually is.

There is so much suffering. Yet so much is self-inflicted through simple lack of curiosity or deep questioning. We take so much for granted, we take so much, we take. Freya came 'back' to me after I moved up the coast aways. I told her I would come and get her one day. She moved the date forward I guess. Swarming at summer solstice, moving up here at spring equinox, she has a sense of timing beyond my ken. I am moved by her resilience, encouraged in my elder years by her ability to do what it takes to keep it together. We know how to take risks, she and I.

I left Green Gulch Farm because life was too comfortable, I fit in so well as the rebel monkey monk and was sure to get ordained. I left the monastery and went feral with only a smidgen of regret, which fell away once I opened that first hive. Everything I had learned about stillness and mindfulness came to bear in that moment. Dozens of bees flew up in my face and, finding me friendly, simply went back to their comb.

Since then I have tried to leave them of course. I am a monk, a wondering wandering monk, not a householder or owner of land. Reluctantly, after taking a year off to travel from sea to shining sea again, I resumed the design of this hive and eventually had that aha! moment of the spiral in the internal space. The hive deepened, became more refined. You can see the influence of the Golden Mean and the Fibonacci scale in its proportions. It pleases the eye as it apparently pleases Great Bee.

Great Bee has high standards. Soul has high standards. Neither can tolerate fragmentation or unkindness for very long. Children who are not loved at all die of this. Bees that are not respected may have to leave. In our world, a world of kindness, thoughtfulness and symbiosis, quality outshines quantity as surely as Stars shine upon us all.

The Divine sent us a messenger should we care to listen: It is time for all of us to leave the Feast and come into our Hearts. This is where we truly meet Beauty. Freya is right here. Hmmm. Welcome home.

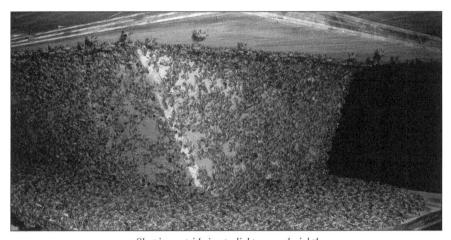

Sleeping outside in starlight ~ good night!

GREAT WISDOM BEYOND WISDOM HEART SUTRA

Avalokiteshvara Bodhisattva when practicing deeply "Prajña Paramita" per-ceived that all five skandhas are empty in their own being and was relieved from all suffering.

"O Shariputra form does not differ from emptiness emptiness does not differ from form that which is form is emptiness that which is emptiness form the same is true of feelings perceptions formations consciousness

O Shariputra all dharmas are marked with emptiness they do not appear nor disappear are not tainted nor pure do not increase nor decrease therefore in emptiness no form no feelings no perceptions no formations no consciousness no eyes no ears no nose no tongue no body no mind no color no sound no smell no taste no touch no object of mind no realm of eyes until no realm of mind-consciousness no ignorance and also no extinction of it until no old-age-and-death and also no extinction of it no suffering no origination no stopping no path no cognition also no attainment with nothing to attain a Bodhisattva depends on Prajña Paramita and the mind is no hindrance without any hindrance no fears exist far apart from every perverted view one dwells in nirvana in the three worlds all Buddhas depend on Prajña Paramita and attain unsurpassed complete perfect enlightenment therefore know the Prajña Paramita is the great transcendent mantra is the great bright mantra is the utmost mantra is the supreme mantra which is able to relieve all suffering and is true not false so proclaim the Prajña Paramita mantra proclaim the mantra that says:

Gate, Gate, Paragate, Parasamgate, Bodhi Svaha!"

Gone! Gone! Gone Beyond! Gone utterly Beyond! Enlightenment ah!

(from the Tassajara chant book)

NOTES

1   I have been assured by master beekeepers that this is never the case and simply not possible ~ however…

2   …the only possible way this hive produced a new Queen is by one of the workers doing the impossible. The sterile queen had been in situ for too long for the rearing of a fertile egg left by the first Queen. I opened the hive long after such an emergency Queen would have hatched. The only option left is that one of the Workers went through internal changes to produce a fertile egg which became the third Queen.

3   In winter the bees will poop but not release fluids in the hive. In summer no bees soil the nest.

BIOGRAPHY

Skye was born in London and spent happy years in Scotland before being sent to boarding school which changes everything. Eventually completing teacher training in Theatre, Literature and Religion she turned away from teaching, being too young, and went to work in the theatre industry becoming a sound mixer for musicals that were new to the West End in the early '70s. Restless and seeking a life style that she had no role models for, she went by bus to India on one of the last 'Magic Bus' trips across Asia, through Afghanistan, Iran, Pakistan and into India, where she stayed for four months, living in a hut in Rishikesh by the Ganges. A certain peace arose, yet the yearning for a teacher took her back to England and across the pond to America where she worked in theatre in New York and San Fransisco, learning the hard way about working in a mans' world, back-stage.

Ever seeking Beauty, yet having to deal with prejudice and even cruelty, she eventually quit and became a monk at San Francisco Zen Center in 1988 where she trained, studied and became a gardener when sent to Green Gulch Farm at Muir Beach, close to the Redwood trees. A certain peace arose. Yet that yearning for a teacher moved her along when Chagdud Tulku Rinpoche offered teachings on Death and Dying, subjects dear to her heart. She moved north to become the gardener at Rigzin Ling in 1994 and still holds Rinpoche as her heart teacher though he passed many years ago.

Leaving the Temple life was not easy, but staying was also unrealistic. New ways of being in the world were required and much study ensued. Following this path of Beauty, falling down a few potholes and making a few mistakes, eventually she returned to upstate New York, no longer in show biz, now living the life style of a monk, offering Feng Shui, gardening and counseling, but after the events of 9/11/01 there was no more peace arising. She thought to return to the monastery but there is no going back, another lesson learned.

It is hard to find quiet hours, clear skies, affordable housing, in America. It's the quiet that is most rare. So, finally, she moved back across the pond, this time to Ireland where there is peace arising again. Quiet enough to hear birdsong, clear enough to speak with stars, peaceful enough to deepen meditation, to still the mind. A small patch of field is becoming a garden, the hive is ready for bees. Life is good. Sometimes you just have to be patient.

LINKS

Sam Comfort
www.anarchyapiaries.org

Chris Harp
www.honeybeelives.org

Gunther Hauk
www.spikenardfarm.org

Tassajara
www.sfzc.org/tassajara

Wendy Johnson
www.gardeningatthedragonsgate.com

Rinpoche
chagdudgonpa.org

Skye Taylor
www.temple-hives.ie
www.skye-talk.com

CPSIA information can be obtained
at www.ICGtesting.com
Printed in the USA
JSHW020310101120
9456JS00004B/119

9 780981 575773